Over a period of 30 years the partnership of James Stirling Michael Wilford and Associates became one of the most renowned international architectural practices. This partnership ended with the death of Sir James Stirling in 1992. The exhibition traces the evolution of that partnership into the current practice of Michael Wilford and Partners. Projects featured in the exhibition, which were designed by James Stirling Michael Wilford and Associates and have been completed, are Temasek Polytechnic, Singapore, for 13,000 students and staff, Stuttgart Music School and the Science Library at the University of California, Irvine, as well as Number 1 Poultry, an office building in the City of London under construction. Work by Michael Wilford and Partners includes The Lowry Centre, Salford, combining facilities for visual and performing arts, Abando Passenger Interchange, with two railway stations and a central bus station in Bilbao, the British Embassy, Berlin and four industrial projects for Sto AG in Germany. Alongside the 11 major projects are recent competition entries and schematic designs to illustrate work in progress. The exhibition comprises sketches, drawings, models and photographs to explain the interlocking architectural strategies which underlie the projects and the evolving design philosophy of the practice.

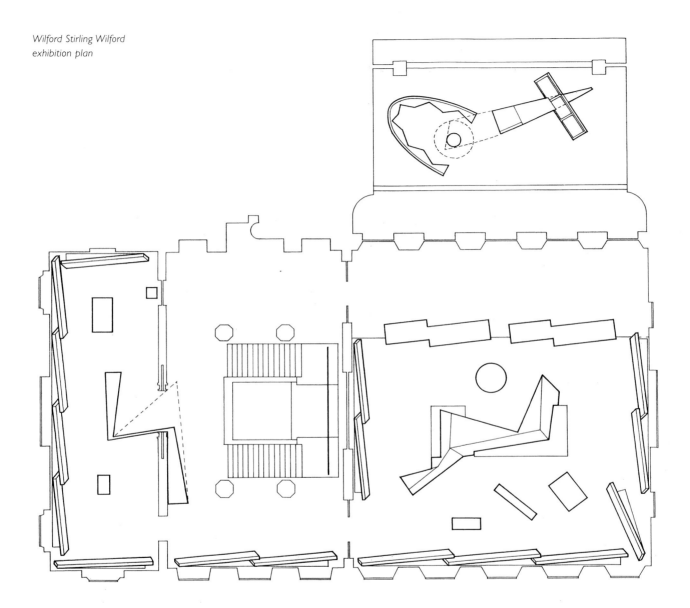

Wilford Stirling Wilford
exhibition plan

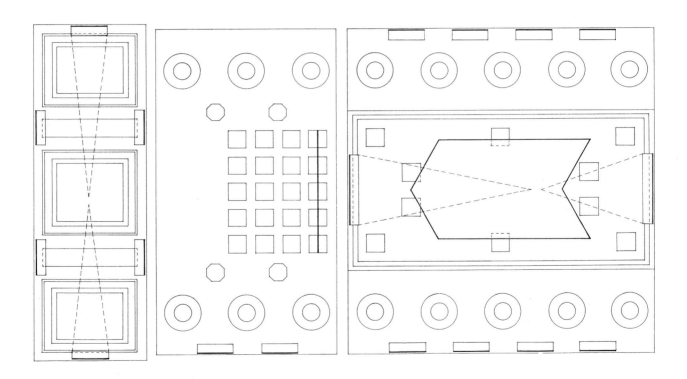

Long section

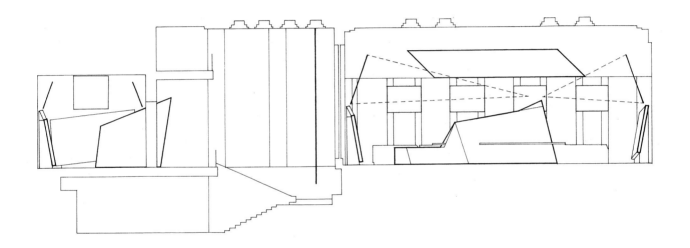

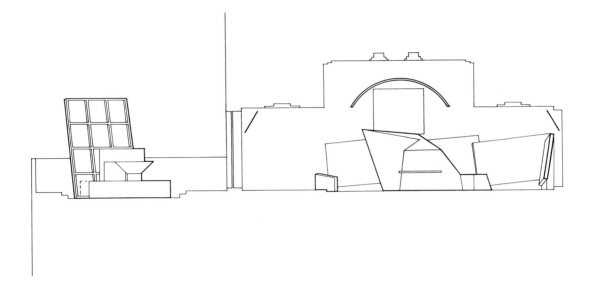

*James Stirling and
Michael Wilford in
the Gloucester Place
office in 1986*

WILFORD

STIRLING WILFORD

Exhibition Design: Michael Wilford & Partners,
Assisted by Thomas Manss & Company, and Mika Burdett
Graphic Design: Thomas Manss & Company
Installation: Benchmark
Lighting Design: Lighting Design Partnership
Lighting: Concord Sylvania

*Published in London to co-incide with the
exhibition 'Wilford Stirling Wilford' at the
RIBA Architecture Centre, 10 June 1996
to 3 August 1996.*

ISBN 1 901050 00 9

CONTENTS

AN EVOLVING DESIGN PHILOSOPHY AND WORKING METHOD

Michael Wilford

Design is an invisible process and it is perhaps understandable that the public have difficulty in comprehending the evolution of the design of a building and the architect's potential contribution to society. From the time that Jim Stirling established the practice, we have always striven to practice architecture as an art, which, as the most accessible and symbolic of the arts, encourages public appreciation through its contribution to the quality of life. Whilst reconciling our parallel obligations to client and society, we are conscious of the profession's responsibility to increase the public's awareness of good architecture and this exhibition is our contribution to this process.

It is curious that the public's sense of an appropriate contemporary architectural style for our pluralistic society can be so heavily influenced by the manifestations of earlier aristocratic and autocratic societies. This anachronism is made even more striking when there exists a simultaneous acceptance of contemporary automobile, aeronautical and communication technologies with a popular appeal for pseudo Georgian homes and Tudor hyper markets. However, truth and significance are not provided by the conventions of appearance.

Architecture, as a pragmatic art, cannot be about style. The battle of style arises substantially from a deep suspicion of change with which modern architecture is associated, particularly negative change, as exemplified by characterless post war housing, banal commercial development and wasted opportunities in the creation of meaningful public space. Confusion between style and quality continues to undermine the development of a truly contemporary architecture in Britain and a distinction has to be made between them in the architectural debate.

An appropriate relationship between our sense of history, the need for stability in our surroundings and the dramatic changes urged upon us by science and technology is as critical now as it has ever been. The arts of literature, drama, music and painting can

Abando Passenger Interchange, Bilbao

individually propose appropriate balances but the architect is more constrained and his power and responsibility often confused in the public mind with developers, planners and other parties over whom the architect often has little influence or control.

Man has always built with aesthetic intention and not only to provide physical shelter. Representing the tastes and attitudes of generations, architecture forms the built stage for human activity and invests man's constructed realm with meaning and value. History tells us who we are and what we have achieved and provides a rich resource of precedents and types to study. As modern architects we have to be conscious of both our social and architectural past and utilise our accumulated knowledge to the benefit of our times.

Through an informed and intuitive understanding, modern architecture can relate to the past and evoke history without compromising authenticity, and achieve a contemporary sense of place, time and continuing tradition. We should interpret by analogy rather than by imitation, thereby transforming and re-charging the meanings of the past. Modernity is not the enemy of history but, by definition, can be nothing but evolutionary. It is concerned with the development of knowledge through a process of research and analysis. Every significant building advances the body of architectural knowledge and the best architects continuously innovate and develop an understanding of the scientific, aesthetic and social aspects of their art.

We are striving to enrich contemporary architecture with a vitality which fuses the Modern Movement's ideals of functionality, clarity, integrity and economy with the traditional qualities of form and space to convey a sense of historical continuity. We are also seeking to maintain a connection between suitability for purpose and beauty.

With some notable exceptions, architecture seems in recent years, to have become divided into two distinct categories, each being overly concerned either with history or technology. We try to avoid such polarities and are interested in exploring a combination of function and technology together with new permutations of the formal and informal. We enjoy incorporating innovative systems and materials while acknowledging our debt to history as part of a broad and profound search for a robust modern architecture which contributes both to the evolution of the city and contemporary culture. People who use and view our buildings have rarely been ambivalent in their reaction to them and we hope to continue to stimulate positive reaction amongst the public at large as well as from the cognoscenti.

We have developed a series of interlocking strategies over three decades of architectural exploration involving:

- The expression of the primary functional activities of the building through a rich, hierarchical composition of formal geometries.
- Incorporation of coherent circulation patterns to provide clear routes and connections in and around the building.
- Development of spatial sequences to reinforce the circulation patterns and functional activities.
- Articulation of spaces in and around the building to enhance the public realm.
- Subordination of structure and systems to formal and spatial objectives.
- Use of solid and void, light and shade, colour, texture, a limited pallet of materials and landscaping in support of formal and spatial objectives.

The layout and design of the exhibition and its relationship with the spaces which accommodate it are intended to exemplify these strategies and analytical diagrams explain how they manifest themselves in each of the projects.

The majority of our urban work involves the insertion of public buildings into established physical contexts and movement patterns. The projects derive their form and character not only from the immediate functional and physical constraints of the building brief and site, but also through the incorporation and definition of new boulevards, plazas, courtyards and other open spaces to enrich the character of the public realm and provide an appropriate setting for the new building. We also intend that they stimulate a fresh interpretation and commentary on the complexities of the cities in which they are located.

Our objective is to transform pre-existing situations into a rich dialogue between past and present without the use of ingratiating historic pastiche or undue deference to the status quo. It is usually possible, with careful analysis of the existing historic growth and fabric of the city, to enhance what often appears initially to be a bleak urban situation.

We employ different compositional strategies in response to the particular requirements of the brief and the demands or location of the site. As the scale of urban projects grows, so the risk of producing amorphous, inappropriately scaled buildings increases. To counter such risk, we accommodate the major elements of the brief within individual and identifiable forms, which are assembled into three-dimensional compositions containing a clear and appropriate hierarchy. Dependent upon the number and comparative size of these forms, architectural order is either inherent in the manner of their combination or

achieved through the introduction of smaller supplementary organising elements. In this approach, the dominant figures establish the identity of the project while the supporting elements respond to the scale and geometry of adjacent structures or spaces and integrate the new building into its context.

In contrast to the architectural compositions designed for restricted urban situations, a more open expression is given to our suburban and green-field projects. Rather than using abstract planning grids, a clear architectural figure is employed to provide overall integrity and an appropriate hierarchy. Another approach is the use of collage in which major elements of the brief are accommodated in a variety of architectural forms. To respond to objective functional criteria these are positioned within an informal composition and interlocked as required to provide functional connections.

The fragmentation of large projects into assemblages of individual forms could, if not carefully controlled, result in visual complexity and confusion. We therefore employ basic geometric figures and a limited range of materials to ensure compositional clarity and architectural integrity. Elaborations to suit particular aspects of the brief are developed within the basic enveloping figures rather than as additions to them.

Pedestrian circulation is a dynamic and motivating element common to all our projects, and is articulated in sequences of richness and subtlety – the opposite of the free plan approach in which activity and circulation are mixed together within a neutral all-embracing enclosure. The form, scale and proportion of the spaces are developed to suit functional and experiential criteria and arranged in clear sequences to punctuate the circulation routes. Approach, entry and internal movement should flow smoothly and allow spaces to unfold graciously in a clear sequential manner. By the use of arcades, promenades, ramps and grand staircases we guide visitors into and through our buildings, and the combination of clearly defined circulation and functional organisation enables them to be used efficiently whilst providing a unique experience. We believe a building should be sufficiently rich in its form and detail to provide a series of layers through which the visitor can progressively discover and enjoy the building.

No architect, however imaginative, can pursue values which are not shared by his client and the community or within the budget. Significant architecture can only develop from a joint commitment to quality and an understanding of the constraints within which architects have to work. An informed and enthusiastic client can make a significant contribution to the design process. Behind each of our buildings is a particular individual or group, who have taken the time to involve themselves in our work, made the effort to comprehend our ideas, supported us by sharing in the risks and, above all, maintained their confidence during the difficult stage of turning initial ideas and diagrams into architecture. Our most successful and highly regarded buildings are those based on mutual trust and respect between client and designer.

Our preference is to involve our clients in the design process as early as possible as part of a systematic approach in which the brief and design are developed in parallel. For us, evolution of a design is a matter of sequence and priority involving the timely consideration of all pertinent factors to ensure that input is valuable rather than an impediment to the design process. In preference to being overwhelmed with detailed requirements at the outset, our ideal initial brief is as concise as possible, providing only key information such as site details, room sizes and primary functional relationships. Together with discussion to appreciate and understand the client's requirements, this basic information is usually sufficient to commence design and can be supplemented as work progresses.

For us, architectural design is an explicit, reiterative and sequential process. Initially all aspirations for the project and constraints upon it are reviewed with the client and a wide ranging diagrammatic exercise carried out to establish all possible ways of configuring the building (or group of buildings) within the constraints of the brief and site. Functionality is always a fundamental consideration in generating the initial diagrams because it is essential that the building performs its required task efficiently. The diagrams are summarised in basic plan, section and three dimensional sketches or models to enable us to consider their validity and compare one to another.

Each alternative is analysed to achieve, through integration and elimination, a progressive narrowing of the range of options, until a basic concept is established which satisfies the brief and which we are confident has architectural potential. The concept thereby results from a myriad of ideas generated by our design teams and prioritised under the guidance of the partners. Our clients' participation in editing the alternative diagrams enables us to better understand their aspirations for the project, allows them an insight into the potential opportunities and involves them in the choice of the concept which will form the basis of the design.

The selected concept is then developed through a series of abstract drawings to indicate the organisation and massing of the project and form the basis of an architectural proposition which will be developed during the schematic design stage. These drawings provide few clues as to image and detail, and patience is required by the client to await the later production of more informative drawings which will reveal the character and appearance of their building.

We communicate all our ideas through the medium of drawing because graphic exploration is fundamental to our design process. We believe drawings allow the best appreciation of a building's intellectual and spatial order, because they focus attention on the essence of a design, and enable comparisons and decisions to be visually informed. Because we think and invent as we draw, we do not use computers during this creative stage. Our use of computers is reserved for technical development and the preparation of production documents once the design is resolved.

The design drawings used to illustrate the projects in this exhibition are a selection of images generated by the office during each project's development and presentation stages. They comprise up and down axonometrics, isometrics and perspectives, as well as orthographic plans, sections and elevations. All are hand drawn to scale, in black ink-line and their appearance is consciously restrained to convey relevant information clearly. In order to allow the eye to encompass the whole image and avoid the incorporation of extraneous information, the drawings are made to a scale appropriate to portraying the desired information. Overlays are used to progressively pare down the scope and detail of an image and that which remains is considered the minimum necessary to convey the maximum information. The drawings represent an architectural understanding of the building as distinct from an impression of how it might look in reality. Despite the apparent consistency of style and technique, the exhibited drawings are the product of many architects working in the office.

Axonometric drawings demonstrate the spatial and volumetric composition of a design in one image without distortion and give an accurate reading of a building because the vertical and horizontal planes are represented at the same scale. A single image of this kind conveys the essence of an idea in a manner which orthographic projection can only achieve with several images and often with less clarity. In addition to general compositional and spatial drawings, components and special elements are also developed and reviewed through exploratory three-dimensional images.

To avoid distortion or misrepresentation, our use of perspective drawings is limited. Models are used in place of exterior perspectives, interiors are represented by one-point perspectives, prepared during the later stages of design. They enable us to study the surfaces enclosing the space and ensure that lighting, air conditioning and other details are properly integrated. Sometimes such perspectives are elaborated and used for presentation purposes, using shading, hatching or dotting to communicate form and surface but they are kept free of gratuitous or fictitious embellishment.

Our use of true-to-scale massing models to assist in the editing of initial design options and to explain them to clients is increasing in parallel with the size and complexity of the projects. We are also more frequently using models to investigate spatial connections and transitions as well as for the development of detailed technical components and elements of construction. We regularly produce larger scale detailed working models of interiors to study, for example, lighting or the acoustic characteristics of a space. The majority of models used for presentations and included in the exhibition were commissioned from model makers working to drawings specially prepared by us for this purpose.

Our design process has been refined over many years and involves contributions from the whole staff. Jim and I were especially fortunate to gather around us talented and dedicated architects necessary to make it work. Key members of staff have been with us for many years and continue to play pivotal roles within the practice. Our long-established commitment to team work has helped us overcome the loss of Jim Stirling and provides a rigorous working method which we continue to review and develop.

PEOPLING IDEAS

John Welsh

When Sir James Stirling died at the age of 68 in 1992, a number of architects and critics suggested that the practice, James Stirling Michael Wilford and Associates, should be closed down immediately. Of course, the comments were not serious but a way of asking if the international reputation of the practice could continue after the death of its founder and most ebullient partner.

Such a measure, if it had been serious, would have been an act of folly. Within 48 hours of Stirling's death, his architectural partner, Michael Wilford told me that he had spoken to all of the practice's clients whose chief concern, beyond their sadness, was to reassure Wilford of their continuing support. Was he supposed to have told them that service had been discontinued in mid-term? Architects are renowned for their high principles but that one seems to be going a little too far.

And such a measure ignores the people who work in any practice. When James Gowan and Stirling split in 1964, one young student remained with Stirling. That was Wilford. Thirty years later, Wilford's partners and associates are the architects who worked on the seminal projects and buildings that have defined the practice and earned it its reputation over the years.

It was Russell Bevington and Peter Ray, the former now a partner, the latter an associate, who both worked on the Stuttgart Staatsgalerie. Laurence Bain, another partner, worked on Number 1 Poultry. Manuel Schupp worked on Number 1 Poultry and the Music School and is now the associate in the Stuttgart office. And Charlie Sutherland, Chris Dyson and Andrew Pryke, three other associates, were all instrumental in the Bibliotheque de France (1989), Tokyo International Forum (1989) and Kyoto station competitions, three projects that produced the strongest new ideas for the practice in the last few years before Stirling's death.

Four years later, Michael Wilford and Partners, the name for the post 1992 practice, not only continues but flourishes. The practice continues to be very successful in terms of workload and range of work. The situation is doubly ironic in that James Stirling Michael Wilford and Associates' quieter times were in the 1980s, when so many architects boomed, while Michael Wilford and Partner's successes have dominated the hungry 1990s. But neither James Stirling Michael Wilford and Associates nor Michael Wilford and Partners has ever been judged on statistical evidence. Instead, their fame rises from pure architectural facets, such as ideas, drawings and buildings.

The question, therefore, is not about the before and after of the dreadful event of 1992, when Stirling died unexpectedly, but whether the culture of James Stirling Michael Wilford and Associates has been smoothly absorbed into the character of Michael Wilford and Partners. As Michael Wilford himself puts it, 'we want to show no sudden change in direction' but continuity and evolution. That is the theme of this exhibition, a display of 17 projects, some designed before 1992 and some after 1992.

But continuity and evolution could just as easily be used to define the two characteristics that dominated James Stirling Michael Wilford and Associates. The practice belonged to a postwar generation of architects, critically analytical of the international style. Its work, in contrast, was characterised by its ability to reflect and build on the direction of its architecture over time.

The work of the 1970s, for example, reflects, among many other factors, a contemporary interest in buildings as megastructures that are infinitely extendible. The all glazed facade of the Florey building, Oxford (1966) was an expression of the insularity of college life, but just one aspect of these student residences. Five years later, the great glazed facade of the Derby Civic Centre project (1970) and Arts Centre for St Andrew's University (1971), had become the defining element of both projects, providing both street front, circulation and civic space. Within ten years, James Stirling Michael Wilford and Associates' architecture enjoyed quite a different character.

Its entry for the National Gallery extension, London (1984) and design for No 1 Poultry (1985) reflect a city increasingly ill-at-ease with modern buildings and a profession seduced by the pictorial qualities of post modernism. Michael Wilford argues that each building differs because of client, brief, context and budget. But the reality is a practice where change of personnel, the vicissitudes of architectural tastes and the development of ideas is the very human explanation of such change.

James Stirling Michael Wilford and Associates managed to balance an innovative architecture with a referential one. A practice that took critically analytical positions against the anonymity of the international style could only do so firm in its knowledge of architectural history. The auditorium of Leicester University Engineering Building (1959) makes an explicit reference to Constantin Melnikov's Workers Clubhouse in Moscow (1926). And Stuttgart's Staatsgalerie with its play on the organisation of circulation at Schinkel's Altes Museum.

Over the years, however, James Stirling Michael Wilford and Associates certainly added one extra dimension. Since its work became canonic so quickly, the practice made reference not only to earlier architectural greats but also to its own work.

Take Temasek polytechnic, started in 1991 and completed in 1995. It provides examples of such references both on the macro-scale of planning and micro-scale of detail. The horseshoe-shaped plaza that welcomes students and orientates them across the site echoes a similar form at the core of the Florey, Derby city centre and Bayer Research Centre, Monheim (1978). At a smaller scale, the strips of neon lighting inserted in star-like patterns into the ceiling of the Staatsgalerie's reception reappears in the linking pavilions of Temasek.

But any comparison between the earlier James Stirling Michael Wilford and Associates and today's Michael Wilford and Partners must examine whether the ability of James Stirling Michael Wilford and Associates to evolve and continue has carried on smoothly. What better way to do so than through the buildings and projects completed before and after Stirling's death.

The process inevitably starts with three buildings from the 1980s – No 1 Poultry in the City of London (1985–1997), the science library of the University of California at Irvine (1988–1994) and Stuttgart's music school (1988–1996). The three provide a snap shot of an era when James Stirling Michael Wilford and Associates' obsession with form and function had been replaced with an interest in place making.

Lord, then Peter, Palumbo had turned to the practice to build a new building in the city after his earlier design by Mies van der Rohe had fallen victim to the public's distaste with modernist towers. The new building had to deal with a hysterical planning mood, reinforced by Prince Charles increasingly vociferous comments. James Stirling Michael Wilford and Associates' building reconfirmed the street plan and reinforced the street scale. Ten years later, the building is now under construction.

The library at Irvine dealt with a different set of circumstances – a disparate campus so characteristic of the 1960s. But the new building makes order of this clutter, drawing people into a circular, central courtyard. Stuttgart's music school, like the earlier Staatsgalerie, also makes sense of a 1960s' disaster – Adenauer Strasse, the local motorway. But this time place and character are not achieved with a void but rather a tower – Stirling, himself, said that the music school's tower was a champagne cork that had blown out of the Staatsgalerie's courtyard.

All three have much in common. There is the use of a circular element at the core – either as an organising element or a strong geometric symbol – running smoothly into linear wings. Each has a generic elevation composed of a grid of windows, nicely and neatly assuming urban good manners. But most importantly all three are expressed in a post modern idiom, not extreme, like some of the practitioners of the 1980s, but post modern all the same.

Then something happened. In 1989, James Stirling Michael Wilford and Associates was among twelve other practices invited to enter the Bibliotheque de France, a competition to design a new national library in Paris. Gone was the post modernism of the 1980s to be replaced by a new vision of buildings expressing strong geometric forms, arranged like an architectural village.[1]

The library's reference library and reading room were placed within a hall with a barrel vaulted roof, corrugated in section. Reading rooms and other public rooms were accommodated within individual buildings and administative offices within a tower, octagonal and cruciform in plan. It was exciting and original, the forms getting yet stronger with two other competition entries – the Tokyo International Forum, 1989, and the Kyoto railway station competition, 1991.

James Stirling Michael Wilford and Associates did not win the competitions but the effort was not wasted. What the practice did achieve, however, was

1. Jenkins, David. RIBA Journal, September 1993, page 53.

the next step in its architectural vocabulary, as important as any of the others since the early 1960s. And each element began to appear in new commissions.

The first project to express such forms was Temasek Polytechnic in Singapore. This new university, completed earlier last year, accommodates 11,500 students and 1500 staff, in departments for applied science, technology, business and design. Teaching blocks, offices and faculty residences are all ordered according to a masterplan which places facilities within linear and cluster blocks radiating from a central horseshoe-shaped plaza.

The references to earlier work have already been mentioned. But what represents the new development, inspired by those three competitions, two Japanese, one French, is the reappearance of buildings, in geometric forms such as the library with its cruciform tower rising from a square base, placed in an architectural village.

Equally interesting is the contemporaneous Abando Interchange in Bilbao, Spain and Lowry Centre for Salford Quays. The Bilbao building provides the city with a brand new rail and bus station but also plays an important role in linking the medieval and 19th century quarters of the city, formally divided by rail tracks and roads.

In an early scheme, a glass roof covers the tracks, a tower rising from each end, one rising from a triangular plan, the other from a square plan. The design, as will be built has moved on but the final form, with its roof of scale-like glass panels and towers indicates an equivalent architectural vocabulary.

The Lowry Centre, which has just received lottery funding, is an exuberant collection of forms (expressing the variously sized theatres and galleries inside) rising above the triangular-shaped footprint. Again, functions

within, such as auditoriums, are expressed in the language of those earlier competitions.

It is at this stage of the practice's workload, as represented by this exhibition, that Stirling died. What could or should have happened now? The nature of James Stirling Michael Wilford and Associates had been to change and develop the architectural character of the practice.

With the death of such an important member of the team would Michael Wilford and Partners, the new practice, now stagnate, churning out the same types of buildings one after another? Or would the practice continue to evolve its architectural character, as it had before, showing that very essence of the practice could continue without Stirling?

The evidence rests with two projects, one completed since 1992, the other under construction. The first is for Sto, a German paint manufacturer. The commission includes a depot in Hamburg where all elements are located within three, differently-shaped and differently coloured elements: the depot in a white coloured, oblong block; a yellow, barrel vaulted office; a mono-pitch showroom, square in plan and painted red.

A headquarters office for the same company in Baden Wurttemberg boasts equally dramatic forms. There are three elements: a marketing office, suspended over all others, parallelogram in section; an oval entrance pavilion; training facilities slipped in below.

Both hark back to the three competitions of the 1989–1991 era, all three informed by the realities and practicalities achieved with Temasek, Bilbao and the Lowry. But, most importantly, the three reveal a step on and up as well.

There is still the architectural village but what the elements do in plan, they also now do in section –

the marketing offices of the Sto headquarters suspended over the training rooms, the yellow office wing of the Sto depot slung over the showroom.

And even more tellingly is the shape of the elements. First it was the pure geometry of square, oblong, triangle and cruciform in the competitions. But the last three projects take this idea further articulating them into what are abstract forms. It is visually rich architecture without being mere facadism for each object still represents and expresses the function of the particular element within.

What, then, is Michael Wilford and Partners? When Stirling died, commentators and critics quite rightly praised his contribution to architecture. What was too often overlooked was the legacy to the practice of his working methods which allowed ideas to rise and circulate throughout the practice. The work since 1992, the characteristic ability not only to make reference but also to change, shows that such a studio still exists.

I am lucky enough to enjoy more personnel evidence of such continuity. When I first started visiting Stirling in the late 1980s, he sat at a huge table in the middle of the first floor office in Fitzroy Square. To one side sat Michael Wilford at a drawing board. As the relationship between Stirling and myself developed over the years so Michael Wilford became more and more part of the conversation.

Just last month, I sat in that same first floor talking to Michael Wilford about this essay. To one side sat Laurence Bain and Russell Bevington, Wilford's two partners, at drawing boards. Time and again as Wilford and I spoke, Bain or Bevington would raise their heads and comment.

John Welsh, editor RIBA Journal London

MUSIC SCHOOL STUTTGART

1986–1996

The Music School and future Theatre Academy will complete the sequence of public buildings along Stuttgart's 'Cultural Mile' and continue the series of external semi-enclosed spaces opening towards the city, initiated by the Staatsgalerie.

A new raised plaza over a parking garage, framed by the Music School, Theatre Academy and Landtag building, is the focus of the urban composition. The L-shaped plan of the Theatre Academy will also enclose a garden opposite the State Theatre and an avenue of trees will complete the leafy promenade along Konrad-Adenauer-Strasse.

Eugenstrasse will be closed to traffic and landscaped to provide an axial pedestrian connection linking the new Theatre Garden to Eugensplatz on the hill above. A footpath between the Music School and Theatre Academy connects the plaza to Eugenstrasse and a broad ramp curving around the base of the tower allows pedestrian and VIP vehicle access to the plaza from Urbanstrasse.

In 1992 the site was divided by the client into two phases; beginning with the construction of the Music School, to be followed by consideration of alternative uses for the Theatre Academy building as the second phase. A decision is yet to be made and in the meantime the urban ensemble remains incomplete.

The Music School comprises nine floors of teaching and practice rooms accommodated in a linear building fronting Urbanstrasse. This is sub-divided into a series of building elements relating in scale to adjacent buildings. The focus of the building is a cylindrical tower containing the Concert Hall and Library, topped by a roof terrace with magnificent views over the city, and giving the building a unique presence on the city skyline. Its vertical windows and coved cornice make reference to the Staatsgalerie rotunda and contribute to the city's rich collection of towers.

Entrances are from the plaza or Urbanstrasse

which is marked by a glass and steel canopy. They lead into a grand multi-level foyer extending across the depth of the building, connecting plaza and street levels to the corner refectory. The public entrance to the Concert Hall is directly from the plaza. Stairs and lifts rise and descend from the foyer to all levels. An exhibition gallery with showcases for musical instruments and manuscripts extends along the length of the building at library entrance level and leads to the Orchestra Rehearsal Room.

The Music School mirrors the Staatsgalerie by continuing the sandstone, travertine and stucco wall finishes and through its formal/informal composition. Axial planning and diagonal movement produce a dynamic balance between the open-air circular court of the Staatsgalerie Rotunda and the Music School Concert Hall Tower.

Whilst the facades of the Staatsgalerie and Kammertheatre comprise walls with few windows, the exterior of the Music School has numerous windows to teaching and rehearsal rooms. The apparently random window pattern relates to the varied size and position of rooms and is visually ordered by a grid of stone pilasters applied to the stucco facades.

Client: Staatlches Hochbauamti, Stuttgart. **Accommodation**: Facilities for 1,000 students and staff including Concert Hall, Orchestra Rehearsal Room, Library, Seminar Rooms, Recording Studios, Exhibition Gallery, Offices and Student Dining. **Schedule of net areas m²**, total: 20,830, Concert Hall (500 seats) 660, Library 250, Studios, Rehearsal Rooms and Classrooms 600, Dining Room 5,000, Administrative Offices 220, Foyers, Circulation, Support and Ancillary Spaces 460. **Architects:** James Stirling, Michael Wilford and Partners, London and Stuttgart. Kenneth Beattie, Claire Bevington, Russell Bevington, John Bowmer, Birgit Class, Axel Deuschle, John Dorman, Felim Dunne, Klaus Fischer, Axel Funke, Irmgard Gassner, Stephan Gerstner, Susan Haug, Wolfgang Heckmann Bernd Horn, Charlie Hussey, David Jennings, Daphne Kephalidis, Steffan Lehmann, Karin Ludewig, Toby Lewis, Markus Mangold, Esmond O'Brien, Eilish O'Donnell, Peter Ray, Ulli Schaad, Klaus-Jürgen Schnell, Manuel Schupp, Philip Smithies, Andrew Strickland, Richard Walker, Karen Waloschek, Siggi Wernik, Karenna Wilford, Denis Wolf, Eric Yim. **Consultants**: Mechanical Services: Ove Arup and Partners, London and Jaeger Mornhinweg & Partner, Stuttgart. Public Health Engineers: Jaeger Mornhinweg & Partner, Stuttgart. Electrical Engineers: Ove Arup and Partners, London, Ingenieurbüro S Burrer, Stuttgart. Structural Engineers: Ove Arup and Partners, London, Boll & Partner, Stuttgart. Building Physics: Dr Flohrer, Berlin. Acoustics: Arup Acoustics, London, Müller BBM, Munich. Stage Equipment: Biste & Gerling, Berlin. Kitchen Planners: Becker, Stuttgart. Cost Consultant: Davis Langdon and Everest, London. Site Supervision: Michael Weiss, Aachen.

*Plan showing the
Staatsgalerie (left) and
the Music School and
Theatre Academy (right)*

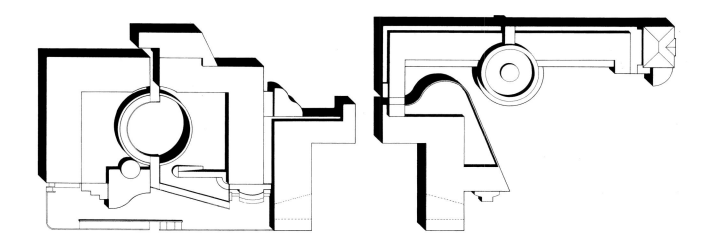

*Elevation to
Konrad-Adenauer-Straße*

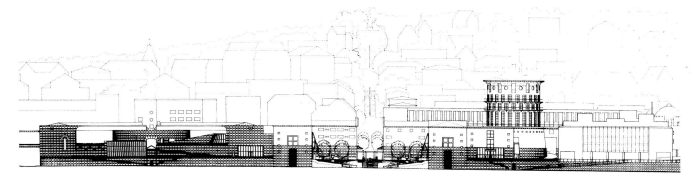

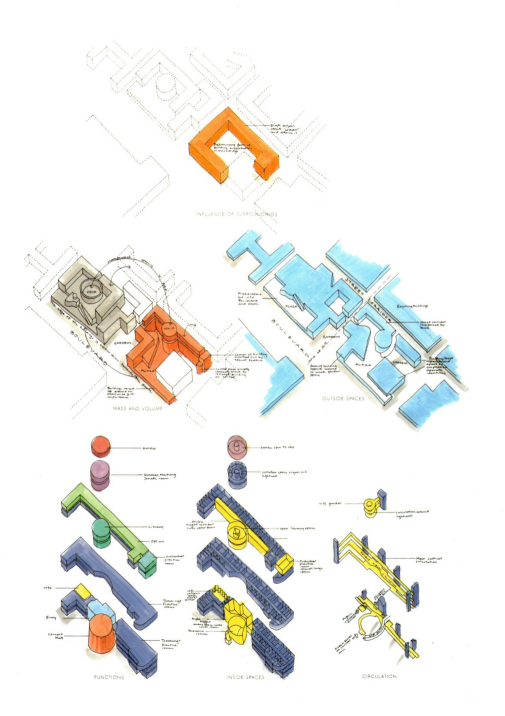

INFLUENCE OF SURROUNDINGS

MASS AND VOLUME

OUTSIDE SPACES

FUNCTIONS

INSIDE SPACES

CIRCULATION

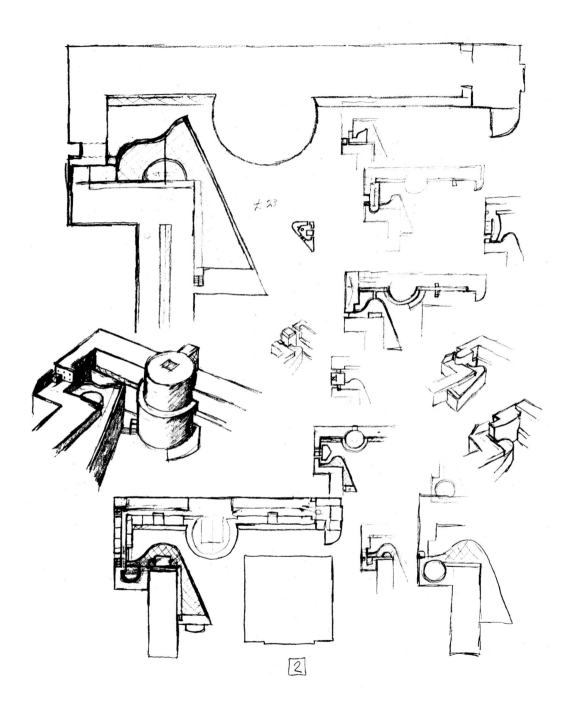

2

Early concept sketches

[3]

Upper teaching rooms and
Senate Room plan

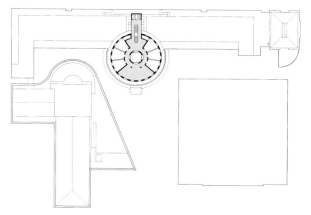

Mezzanine level library plan

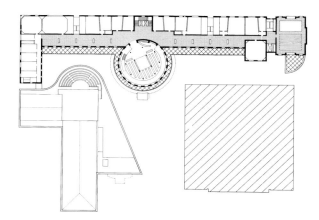

Upper level Concert Hall plan

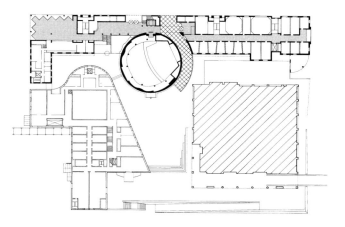

Plaza level plan

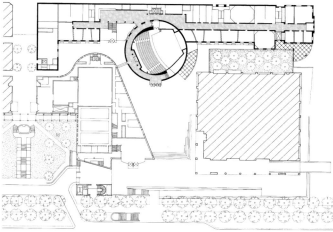

Konrad-Adenauer-Straße
elevation (Staatsgalerie
on the left, Music School
on the right)

Section through Plaza
and Music School.

Section through
Theatre Academy
and Music School

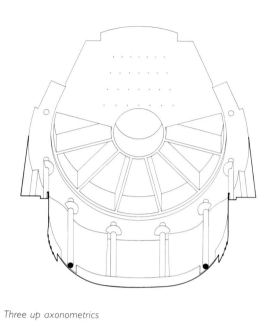

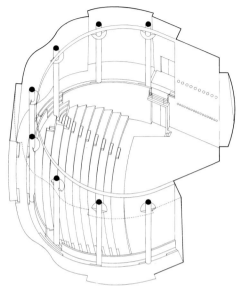

*Down axonometric
showing seating
in concert hall*

*Three up axonometrics
of concert hall*

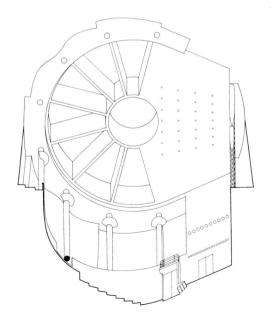

*Sectioned up
axonometric
of library*

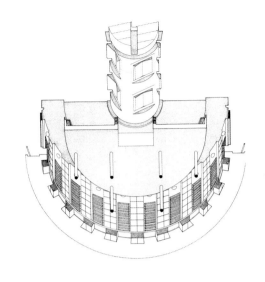

*Down axonometric
of entrance foyer*

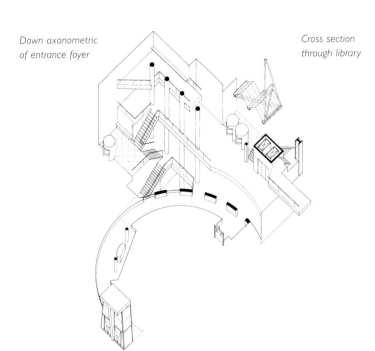

*Cross section
through library*

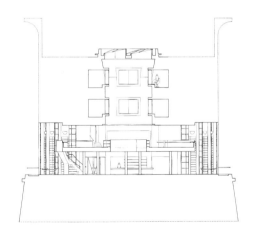

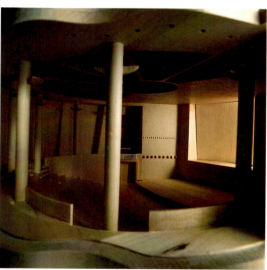

Stuttgart's towers

Tower up view

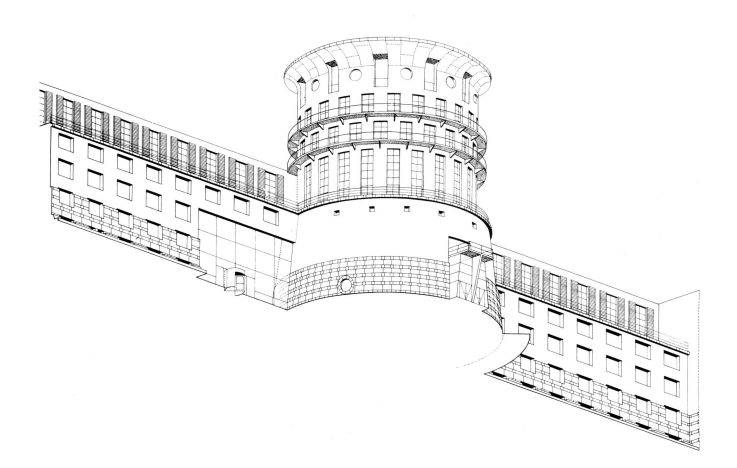

TEMASEK POLYTECHNIC SINGAPORE

1991–1995

Temasek Polytechnic is a 'city of learning' for 11,500 students with 1500 staff, encompassing Schools of Applied Science, Technology, Business, and Design, in a 30 hectare landscaped park between Tampines New Town and Bedok Reservoir at the eastern end of the island of Singapore.

A raised entrance Plaza, enclosed by the horseshoe-shaped administration building and opening towards Tampines Avenue, is the focus of the campus and a public forum representing the Polytechnic's open relationship with the community. A large 'window' through the horseshoe frames panoramic views across a triangular garden to the reservoir. A covered footbridge connects the Plaza to bus shelters on either side of Tampines Avenue.

A promenade with bank, shops, and school entrances in the base of the Administration Building is a contemporary version of the traditional Chinese shop house 'five foot way'. Beneath the plaza, an auditorium and multi-purpose theatre share a public foyer with an entrance from Tampines Avenue.

The four schools are organised along spacious pedestrian concourses radiating from the promenade and sheltered by upper levels of accommodation. The spatial organisation optimises vertical and horizontal movement, with the most densely used spaces such as lecture theatres situated on, or below, concourse level. Each school has its own student canteen overlooking the park.

The promenade, concourses and covered ways through the landscaped parkland, form a weather protected pedestrian network connecting all academic and recreational areas. A perimeter service road links all buildings and car parks with controlled entry gates from Tampines Avenue at each end of the Campus.

The highest building on Campus is the Library Tower which is connected to the administration building, and announces the presence of the

Polytechnic on the Singapore skyline. The Student Centre and Central Canteen are located alongside the triangular garden close to the Sports Hall and Stadium. The Faculty Club and staff housing towers enjoy distant views from higher ground at the western end of the Campus.

Contrasting landscapes of the Plaza Parterre, triangular garden and open park land surrounding the schools and recreational facilities, ensure a variety of experiences, a sense of orientation and unify the campus. Clusters of large trees shade buildings, parking and outdoor study areas. Spaces between and beneath the buildings create air movement across pedestrian zones.

Shadow plan of Temasek Polytechnic Campus

Client: Temasek Polytechnic. **Accommodation**: Facilities on a 30 hectare site for 11,500 students and staff including administration, auditoria, music school, library, schools of applied science, technology, business and design, student centre central canteen, faculty club and child care centre, swimming complex, sports hall and fields and staff housing. **Schedule of net areas m²**, total: 215,000 m², Administration, Music School & Library 32,750, Large Auditorium (600 seats) 700, Multi-Purpose Auditorium (250 seats) 300, School of Applied Science 36,260, School of Technology 70,850, School of Business 20,110, School of Design 14,860, Student Centre & Central Canteen 5,800, Faculty Club and Child Care 2,480, Multi-purpose Sports Hall 6,680 Swimming Complex 1,640, Staff Housing 22,570. **Architects**: James Stirling Michael Wilford and Associates, Laurence Bain, Paul Barke, Russell Bevington, John Bowmer, Mark Bunting, Chris Chong, John Dorman, Frances Dunne, Christopher Dyson, Liam Hennessy, Charlie Hussey, Andrew Pryke, Peter Ray, Leandro Rotondi, Charlie Sutherland, Kit Wallace, Karen Waloschek, Gareth Wilkins. **Consultants**: Architects: Associate Architect: DP Architects Pte, Singapore. Structure, Mechanical, Electrical & Special Services: Ove Arup & Partners, International, London. Mechanical & Electrical Engineers: Ewbank Preece Engineers Plc,Singapore. Structural Engineers: Ove Arup, Singapore. Quantity Surveyors: KPK, Singapore. Landscape: PDAA, Singapore. Acoustics: Arup Acoustics, London, Acviron, Singapore. Project Management: Public Works Department, Singapore.

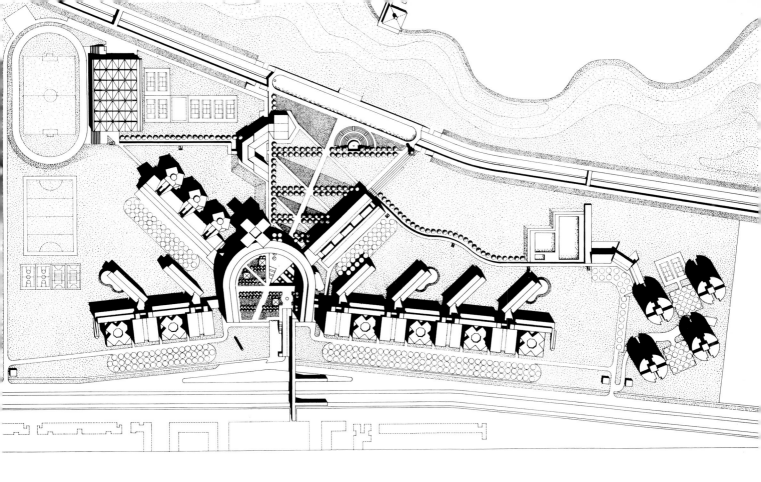

Elevation of School of Applied Science (left), Administration Building and Plaza (Centre) and School of Technology (right).

Section through Central Plaza, Administration Building, Library Tower Student Centre (right

Administration

TEMASEK
POLYTECHNIC
Welcome · 欢迎 · Selamat Datang · நல்வரவு

Alternative site plan studies

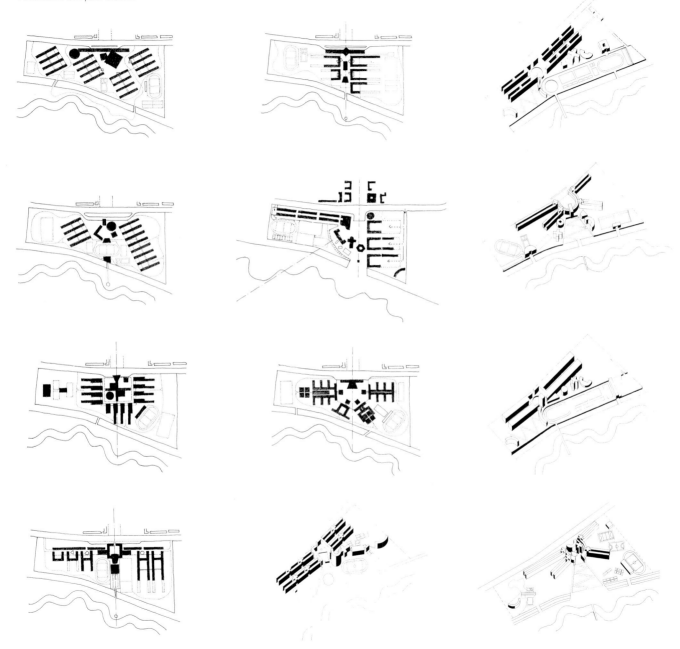

Up axonometric of administration building and library tower

Down axonometric of administration building, library tower and plaza

*Plan of administration
building and library
at upper level*

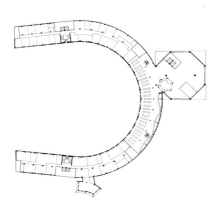

*Typical plan of
administration building
and library*

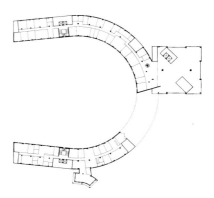

*Plan of administration
building and library
at plaza level*

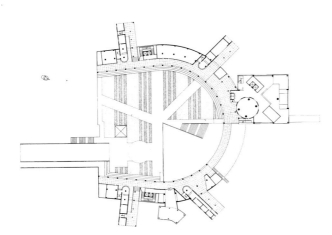

*Plan of administration
building and library
at under-plaza level,
showing theatres
and foyers.*

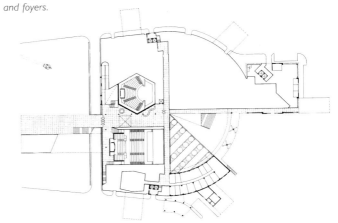

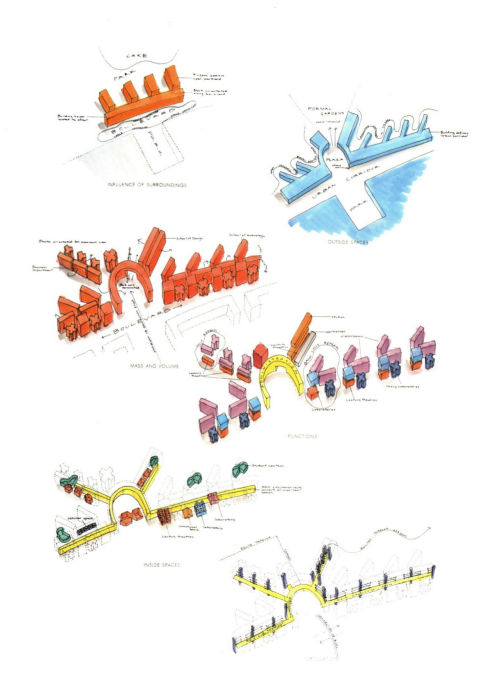

INFLUENCE OF SURROUNDINGS

OUTSIDE SPACES

MASS AND VOLUME

FUNCTIONS

INSIDE SPACES

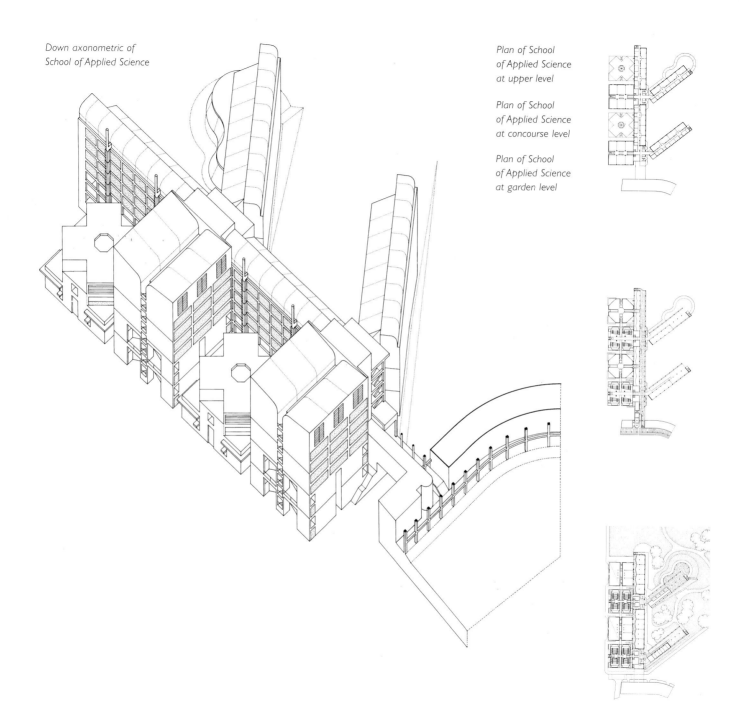

Down axonometric of
School of Applied Science

Plan of School
of Applied Science
at upper level

Plan of School
of Applied Science
at concourse level

Plan of School
of Applied Science
at garden level

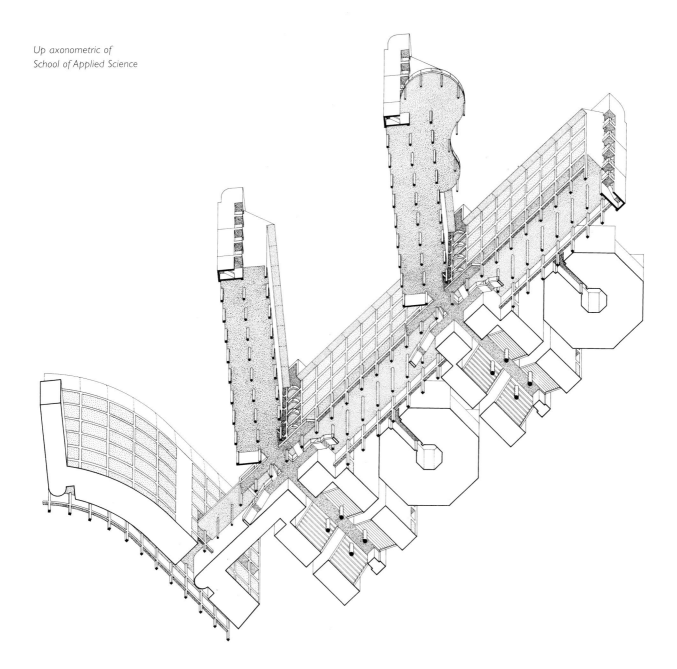

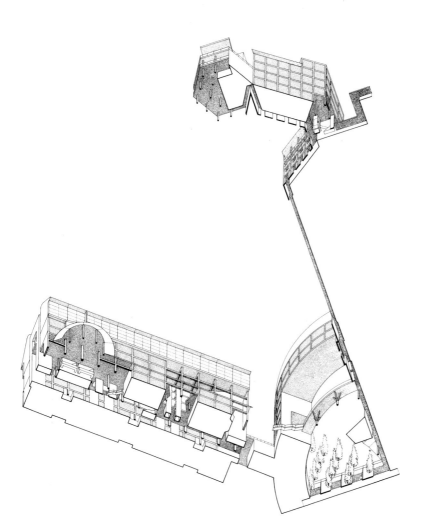

Up axonometric of
School of Design (left),
administration building
(centre) and student
centre (right).

Plan of the School of
Design at studio level

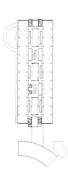

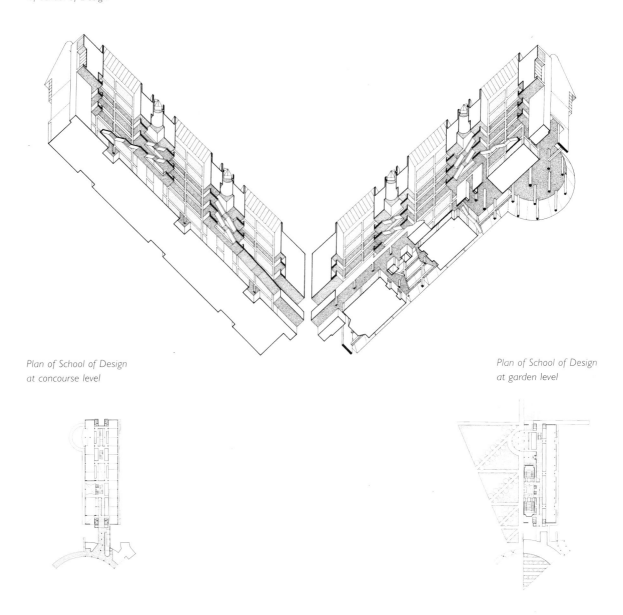

Split up axonometric
of School of Design

Plan of School of Design
at concourse level

Plan of School of Design
at garden level

*Up axonometric of
the student centre*

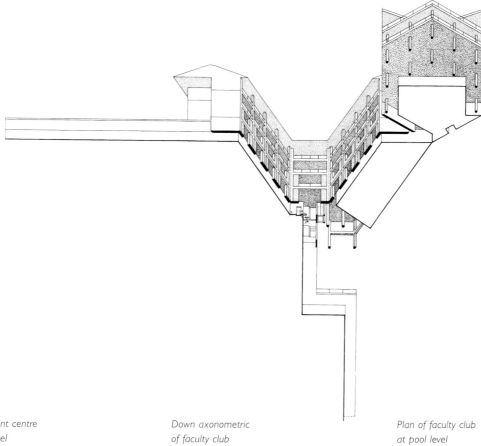

*Plan of student centre
at garden level*

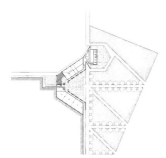

*Down axonometric
of faculty club*

*Plan of faculty club
at pool level*

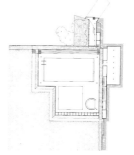

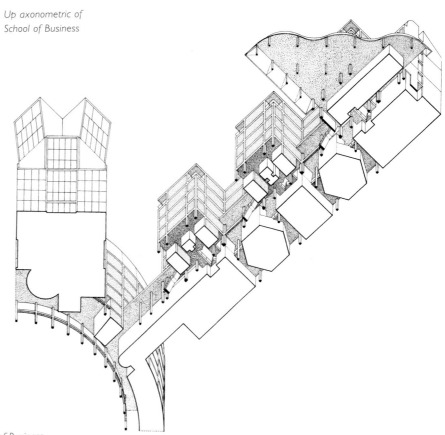

Up axonometric of
School of Business

Plan of School of Business
at typical upper level

Plan of School of Business
at concourse level

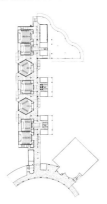

NUMBER ONE POULTRY

1985–

In July 1985, James Stirling Michael Wilford and Associates were commissioned to design a building containing offices, shops and public spaces for a site in the heart of the City of London which was already the subject of controversy. The site is bounded by Poultry, Queen Victoria Street and Sise Lane.

A tower, designed by Mies van der Rohe, which went to public inquiry, was refused planning consent by the Secretary of State. However, in reaching his decision, he stated that he did 'not rule out redevelopment of the site if there was an acceptable proposal for replacing existing buildings'.

By 1986, we had prepared two alternative designs for planning approval, one of which was selected and developed after negotiations with the City of London Planning Office. It occupied a smaller site than that used for the Mies Van der Rohe design, but the earlier furore and concern at the loss of existing buildings, forced another public inquiry.

Following that inquiry, the Secretary of State approved our developed design in October 1988; but the argument continued for more than two years into the propriety of the decision. The House of Lords finally resolved the argument in favour of the design. After a third public inquiry in 1993, agreement was obtained from the Department of Transport to close Bucklersbury, a narrow road which crosses the site.

The design for Number 1 Poultry was determined by existing street patterns and the Bank Junction which is surrounded by several historic buildings, The Bank of England (Soane), The Midland Bank (Lutyens), and St. Mary Woolnoth (Hawksmoor). These historic buildings are symmetrical in plan although they face onto an informal street pattern. Our design for Number 1 Poultry is planned about a central longitudinal axis with similar facades to Queen Victoria Street and Poultry. The parapet height and vertical division of the facades into distinct parts also correspond to surrounding buildings.

The new building contains shops at basement and ground floor levels, with five floors of offices, a roof garden and restaurant above. A pedestrian passage through the building links to an open court, which brings daylight into the centre of the building and to shopping colonnades on the Poultry and Queen Victoria Street frontages. The court, with interlocking circular and triangular plans, extends to basement shopping and the Bank Underground Station below.

Public access to the offices is from the court, with a ceremonial entrance from the apex of the building, via a grand stair to the first floor balcony of the court. Lifts connect the public and private levels of the court and all office floors with the rooftop garden restaurant.

The centre of the garden is enclosed by a circular pergola around the court to form a sanctuary from the hustle and bustle of the city below. Outer gardens provide views of St.Pauls, the Bank Junction and surrounding historic buildings. The building will be faced in sandstone and granite with bronze metalwork.

Client: City Acre Property Investment Trust and Altstadtbau Ltd. **Accommodation**: Mixed use development consisting of offices, retail and roof-top public restaurant. **Schedule of net areas m²**, total: 13,170, Restaurant 500, Offices 10,200, Retail 2,120, Public house 350. **Architects**: James Stirling Michael Wilford and Associates, Laurence Bain, Paul Barke, Andrew Birds, Robert Dinse, Felim Dunne, Frances Dunne, Liam Hennessy, David Jennings, Toby Lewis, Tessa Mahoney, Chris Matthews, Alison McLellan, Alan Mee, John Munro, Jess Paull, Richard Portchmouth, Andrew Pryke, Peter Ray, Brian Reynolds, Leandro Rotondi, Michael Russum, John Ryan, Manuel Schupp, Joanna Sutherland, Simon Usher, Ulrike Wilke, Gary Wyatt. **Consultants**: Structural, Mechanical and Electrical Engineering: Ove Arup and Partners. Quantity Surveyor: Monk Dunstone Associates. Landscape: Lennox-Boyd Landscape Design Ltd. Office Agents: BHz. Shopping Agents: Hillier Parker. Planning Agents: Montague Evans. Architects for the site: Armstrong, Smith and Baron. Facades: Arup Facade Engineering.

Context plan

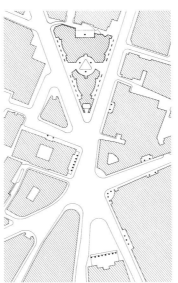

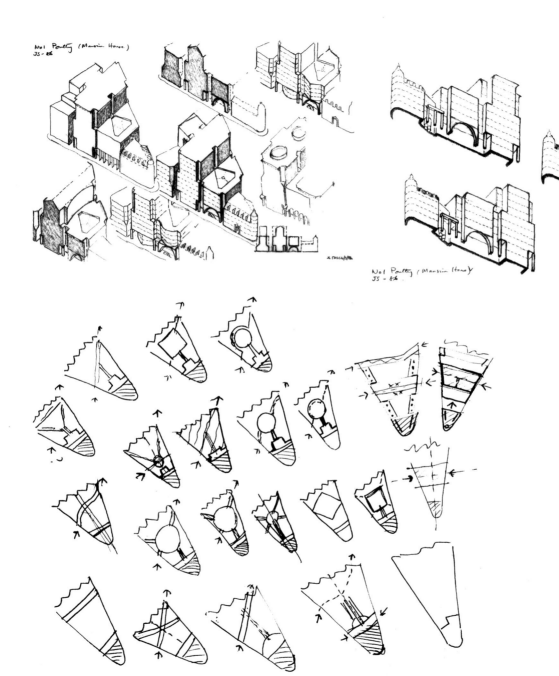

No1 Poultry (Mansion House)
JS - 86

No1 Poultry (Mansion House)
JS - 86

JS - 86

No1 Poultry. (Mansion House)

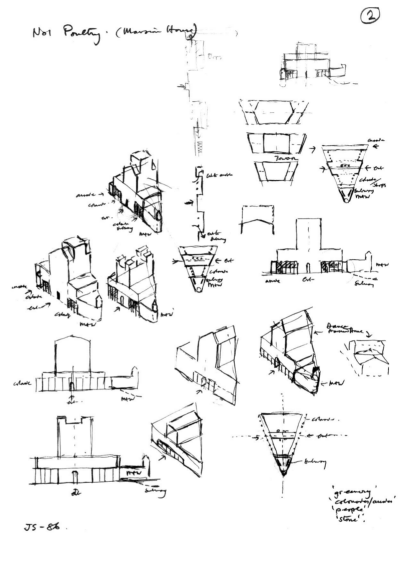

JS - 86 .

'greenery'
'colonnate/arcade'
'people'
'stone'.

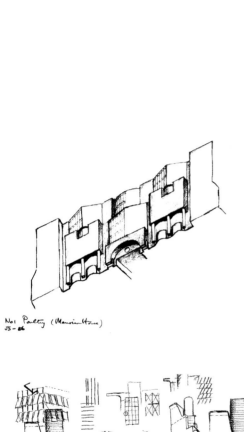

No1 Poultry (Mansion House)
JS - 86

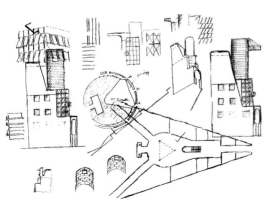

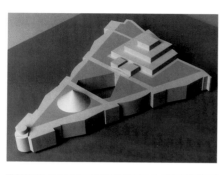
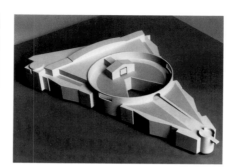
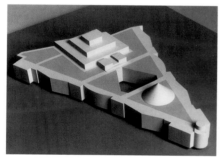
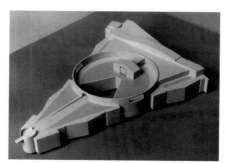
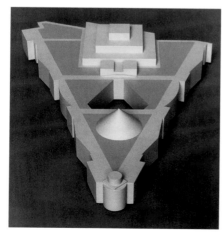
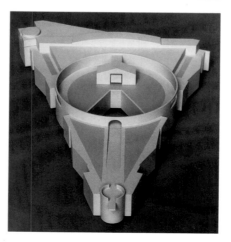

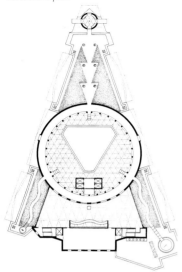

*Roof garden and
restaurant plan*

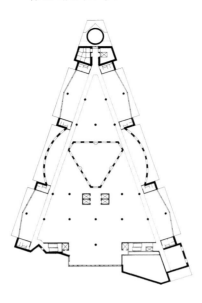

Typical office floor plan

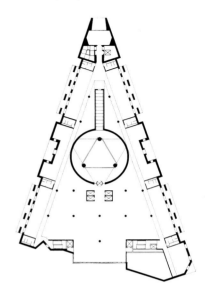

First floor plan

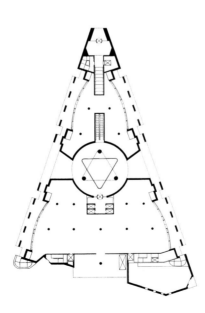

Ground floor plan

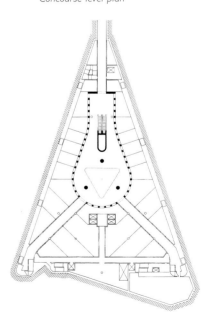

Concourse level plan

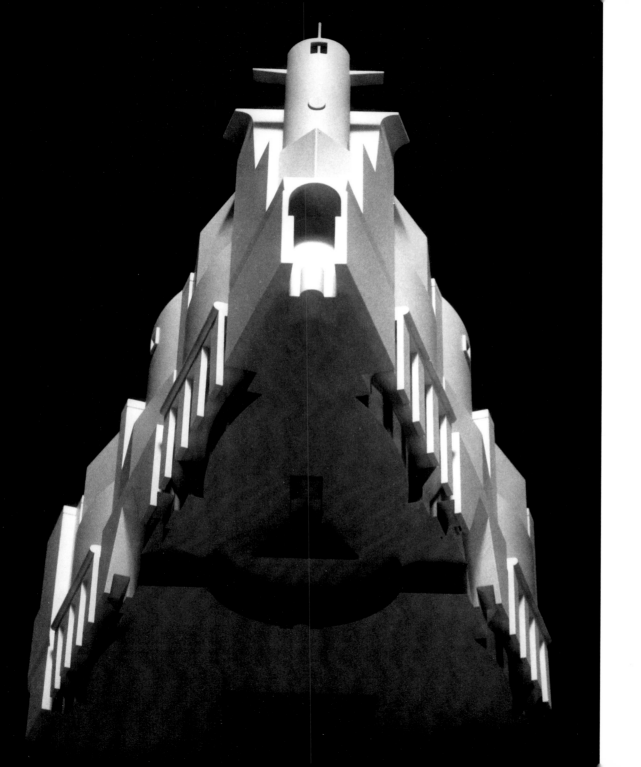

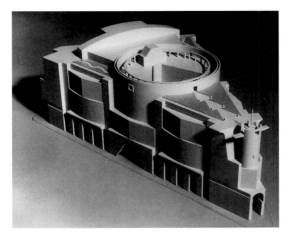
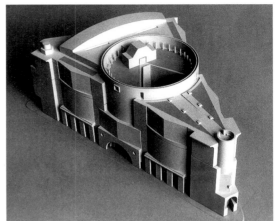

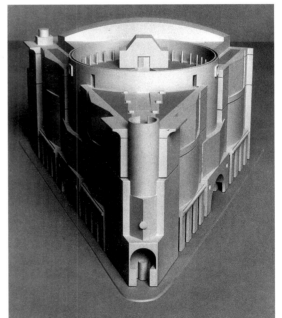

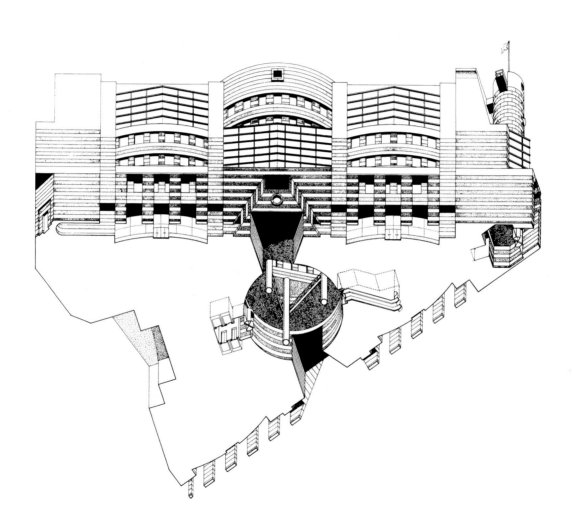

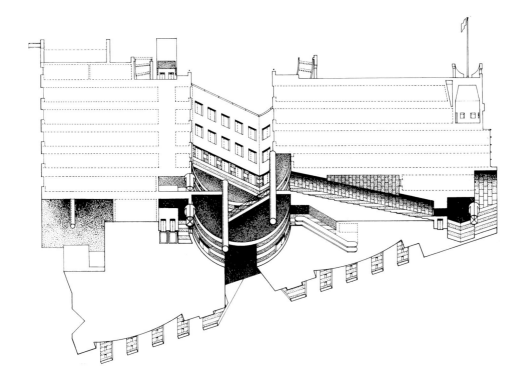

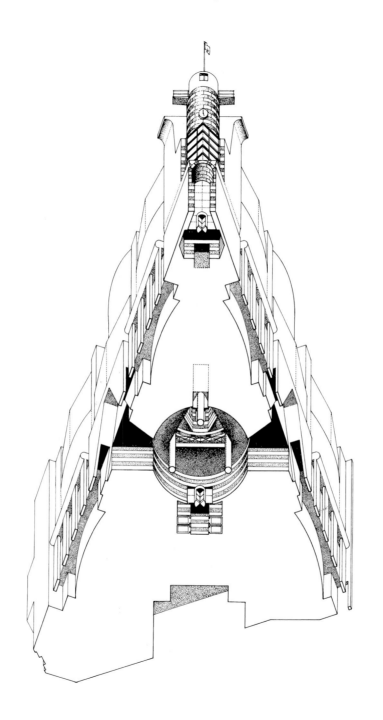

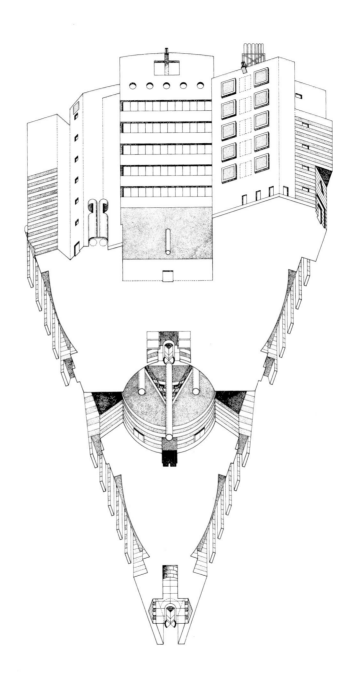

ABANDO INTERCHANGE BILBAO

1992–

The existing Abando Passenger Station and sidings separate the medieval and 19th century quarters of the city and contribute little to the amenity of adjacent neighbourhoods.

The new Abando Passenger Interchange will forge strong connections between the two halves of the city and assist revitalisation of the central area by replacing existing service activities adjacent to the station with business, cultural and residential amenities more appropriate to the city centre location.

It comprises a central bus station for suburban and inter-city bus services, and two new railway stations. The transport facilities are layered and linked directly to the Metro and adjacent streets to provide convenient passenger access and connections. The Passenger Interchange also contains a retail concourse, World Trade Centre, post office, offices, hotel and housing. Removal of the existing station plateau and relocation of the railway stations to the centre of the site, allows construction of a new public plaza and mixed-use buildings along the flanking streets to establish a vibrant new heart to the city.

The new plaza, with covered car and taxi drop-off, is the forecourt of the Interchange. It forms a new centre of social activity and a place for visitors to orient themselves before exploring the city. The dramatic vaulted roof of the Interchange will register its presence on the city skyline. The World Trade Centre tower is the focus of the triangular garden above the rail tracks as they enter the station.

The Passenger Interchange can be entered by pedestrians from all sides and at several levels. The FEVE railway station and retail concourse are situated between the RENFE railway station and bus station. The concourse connects the flanking streets at numerous locations as part of a network of pedestrian routes through the Passenger Interchange, which weave the medieval and 19th Century streets together.

The new RENFE station, situated along the centre of the site at existing track level, contains twelve platforms for long and short distance trains including the new high speed AVE. Trains will emerge from a tunnel into the grand station hall, which is flooded with daylight from the vaulted roof above and provides a dramatic entry into the city. Lifts and escalators connect platforms to all levels and interchange facilities.

Situated between the bus station and RENFE railway station, the new FEVE railway station is the focus of the retail concourse linked by arcades to the adjacent street. The concourse is a place for passengers to buy tickets, relax in lounges, shop in comfort or enjoy refreshments whilst waiting for a bus or train. Escalators connect to the bus stands below and RENFE train platforms above. Inter-city and suburban buses enter the Passenger Interchange via ramps from a motorway spur into a large hall at plaza level, which is connected by escalators, lifts and stairs to the concourse, plaza and streets.

The Passenger Interchange will incorporate existing disparate bus and train passenger termini into one central facility which is linked to the Metro to provide convenient access and interconnection between all modes of public transport.

Client: Estacion Intermodal de Abando, Gestion del Proyecto, SA. **Accommodation**: A new passenger interchange for rail, bus and car with housing, offices, hotel and retail facilities. **Schedule of net areas, total m²**, total: 307,720, Renfe station (15 platforms) 51.590, Feve station (4 platforms) 10,060, Interurban bus station (34 stands) 15,050, Suburban bus station (27 stands) 16,010, Offices 18,340, Housing 48,810, Hotel/exhibition/restaurant 12,060, Retail 18,590, Car parking 43,010. **Architects**: Michael Wilford and Partners, Paul Barke, Darren Capel, Iain Clavadetscher, Chris Dyson, Jeremy Emerson, Kenny Fraser, Christina Garcia, David Haseler, David Jennings, Kirsten Lees, Ian McMillan, John Munro, Manel Pares, Adele Pascal, Andrew Pryke, Brian Reynolds, Jonathan Rose, Simon Whiting Megan Williams. **Consultants**: Architects: Michael Wilford and Partners Ltd. Associate Architects: Deurbe SA. Structural Engineers: Ove Arup and Partners. M&E Engineers London and Madrid. Cost Consultant: Davis Langdon Edetco SA. Cladding Consultants: Atelier One & Arup Facade Engineering.

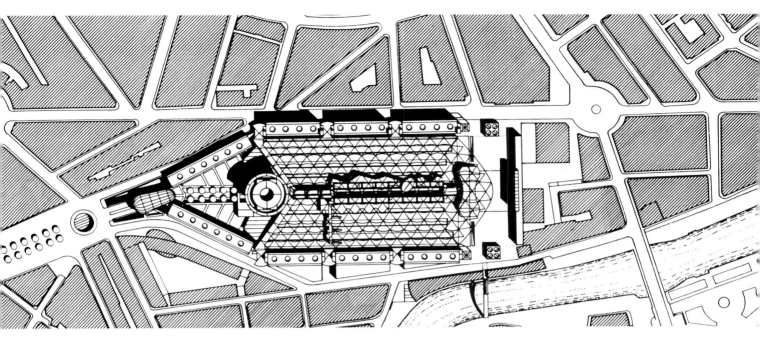

Context plan

Existing city plan

City plan showing
Abando Passenger
Interchange and its
relationship with the
old and new quarters
of the city

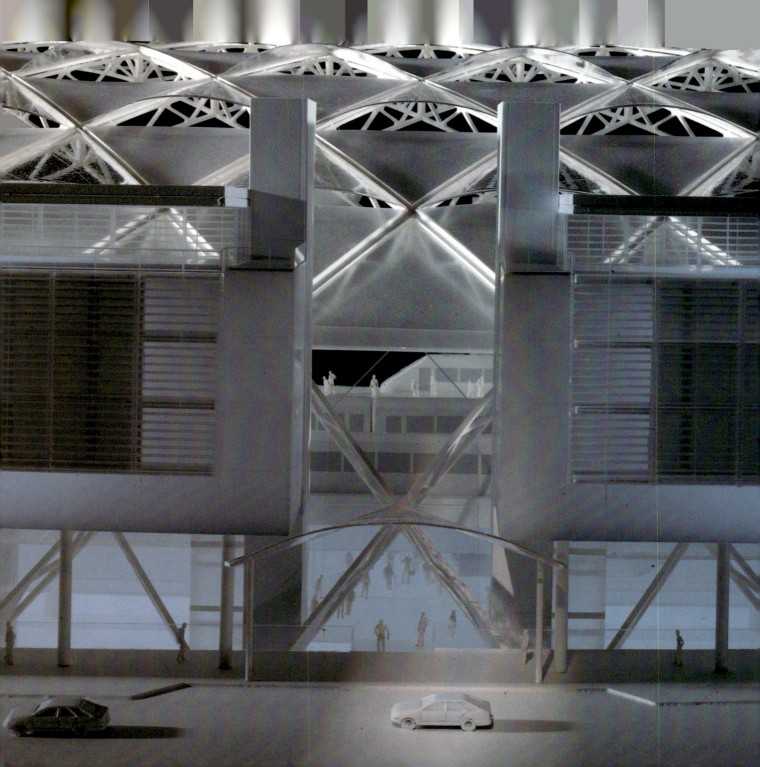

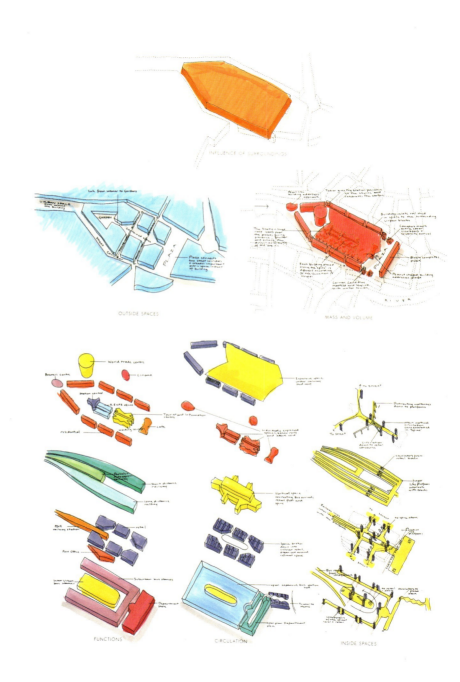

INFLUENCE OF SURROUNDINGS

OUTSIDE SPACES

MASS AND VOLUME

FUNCTIONS

CIRCULATION

INSIDE SPACES

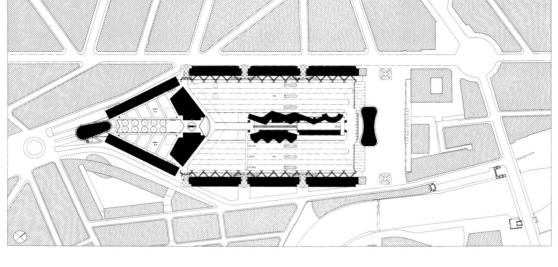

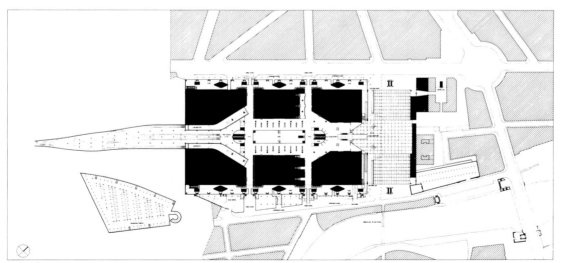

Station level plan

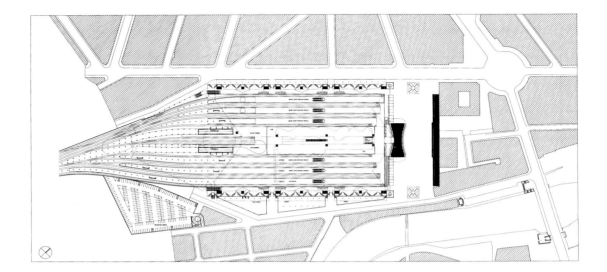

Bus station level plan

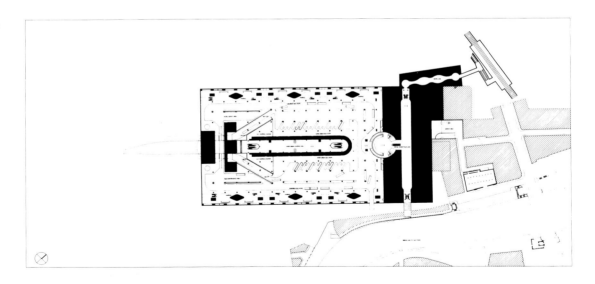

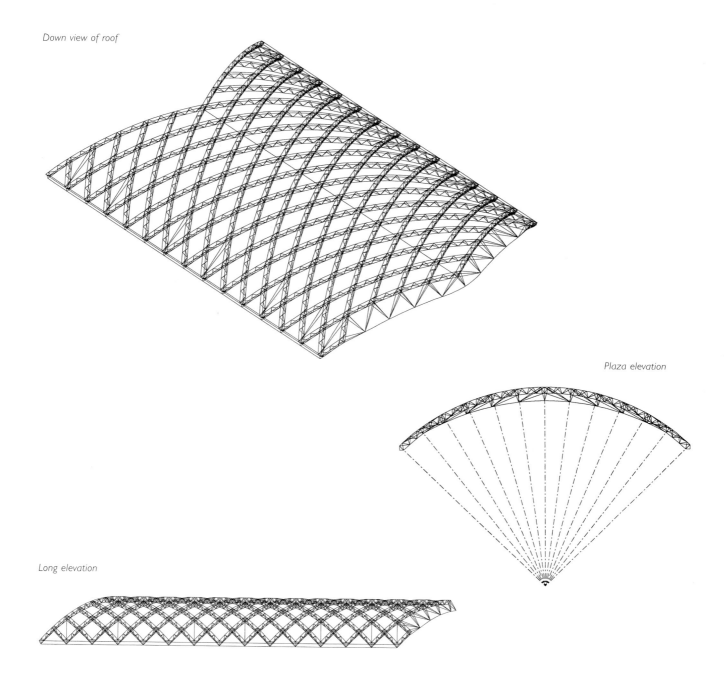

Down view of roof

Plaza elevation

Long elevation

Bus entrance elevation

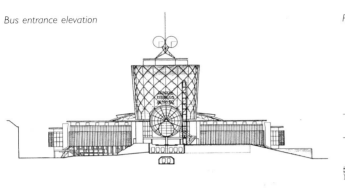

Plaza elevation

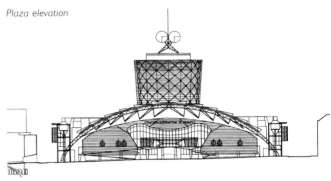

*Cross section through
office tower*

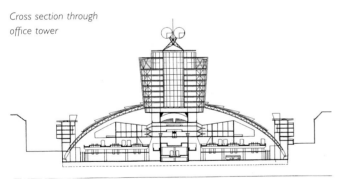

*Cross section through
railway and bus stations*

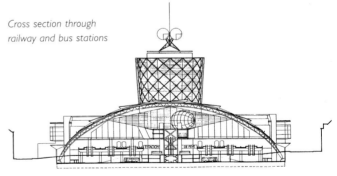

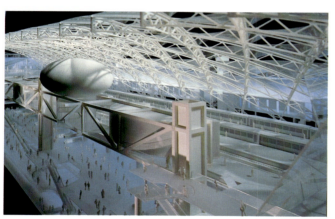

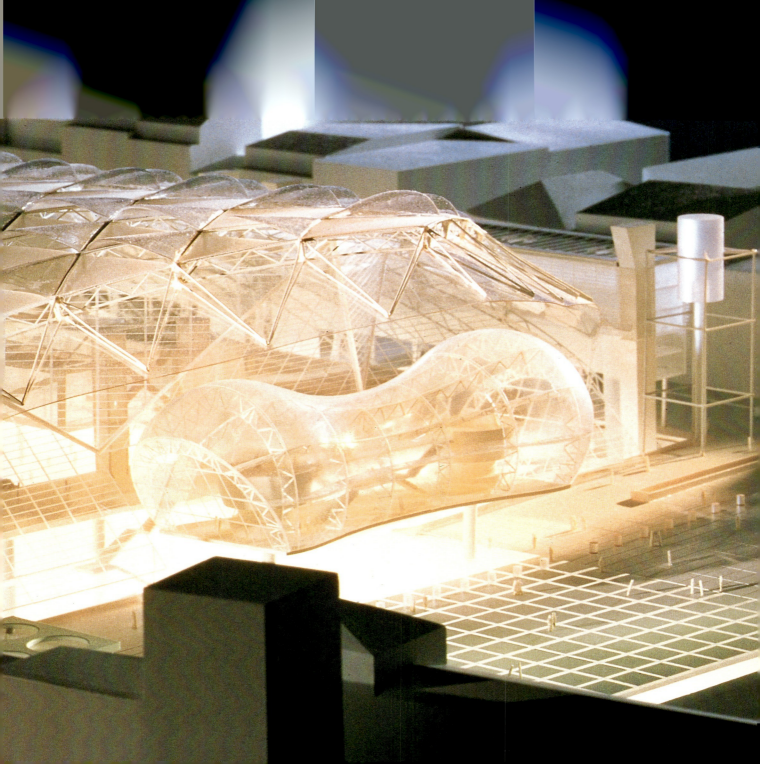

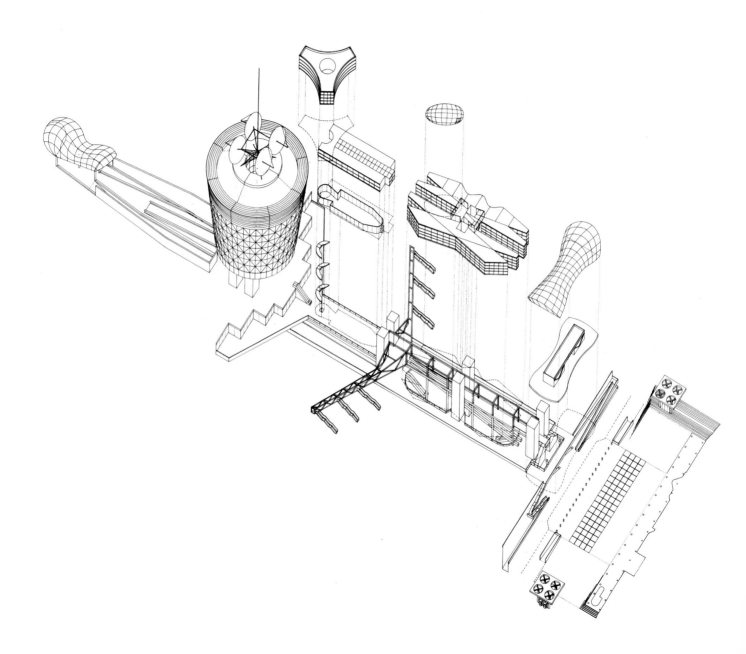

*Exploded down view
of central spine*

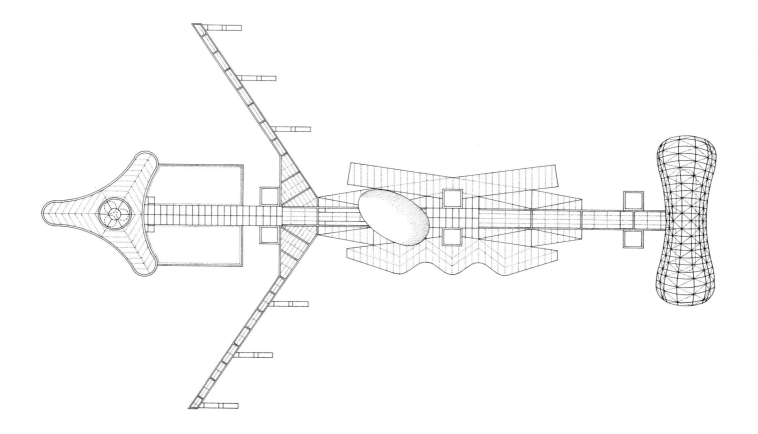

STO HEADQUARTERS WEIZEN

1993–

Sto AG is an international manufacturer of stucco, paints and wall cladding systems based in Southern Germany. Their main production plant, located in Weizen, Baden–Württemberg, is situated on a plateau, enclosed by steep tree-lined hills and overlooking an idyllic river valley.

The company requires larger and more efficient accommodation for administration, production and research. The master plan integrates new and existing buildings into an arcadian campus to satisfy functional requirements within a responsible ecological environment.

Re-routing of the busy road, which currently subdivides the plant, offers the opportunity to unify the separate areas and project the presence and identity of the company to passing motorists through dramatic new buildings accommodating research, marketing and training facilities. A new semi-circular garden for the enjoyment of staff and visitors, and situated across the line of the existing road, is the focus of the campus. Office and laboratory buildings provide a back-drop to the garden and screen the production areas beyond.

A new railway spur and truck route for material delivery and product dispatch encircles the campus, defining a new lake and traffic-free central core.

An axial pedestrian promenade extends from staff car-parking in the valley, across the garden and through the production building to new offices on the opposite side of the campus. A second promenade, at right angles to the first, links offices and laboratories along a garden loggia to the logistics centre.

Visitor reception is centrally located at the inter-section of these promenades, which ensure direct con-nection to all departments. Social facilities will enliven the relationship between the promenades and activity areas, as well as encouraging the staff's interaction and sense of involvement in the company's activities.

The master plan incorporates the company's anticipated space requirements for the next 15 years and allows phased construction of new buildings and reconstruction of many of the existing facilities without interrupting operations.

Existing site plan

Proposed masterplan

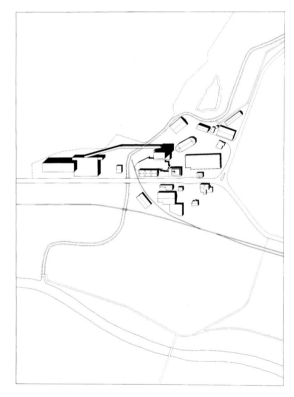

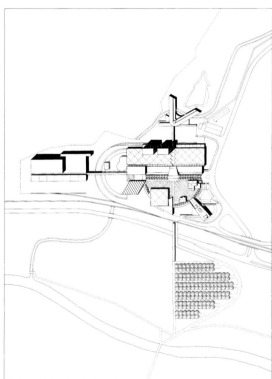

Client: Sto AG. **Accommodation**: New production facility for the manufacture of paint, stucco and render systems, with testing and research laboratories, offices and workshops. **Schedule of net areas m²**, total: 20,150, New production 6,720, Testing laboratories 1,580, Research laboratories 730 Offices (new) 7,950, Workshops & training 2,840, Canteen/social rooms 330. **Architects**: Michael Wilford & Partners, London and Stuttgart. Stuart McKnight, Ian McMillan, Manuel Schupp, Andy Strickland, Charlie Sutherland, Karen Waloschek. **Consultants**: Mechanical & Electrical Engineers: Jaeger, Mornhinweg & Partner, Stuttgart. Structural Engineers Boll and Partner, Stuttgart. Production Planners: OTB, Basel.

Masterplan

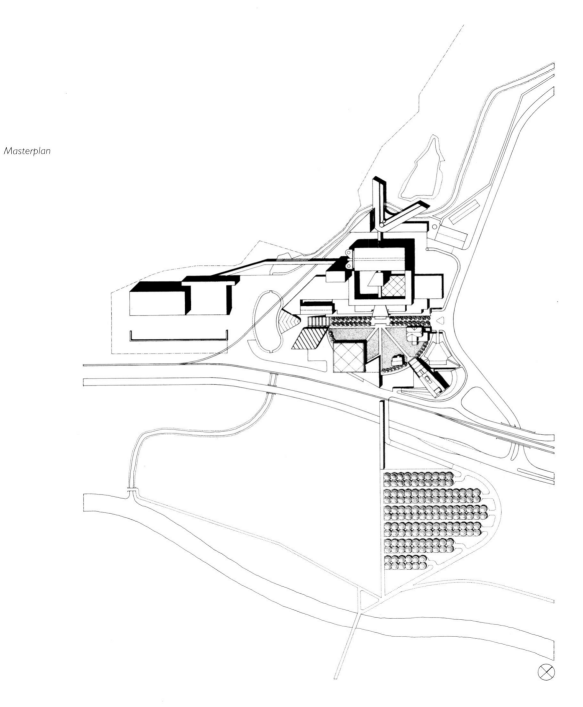

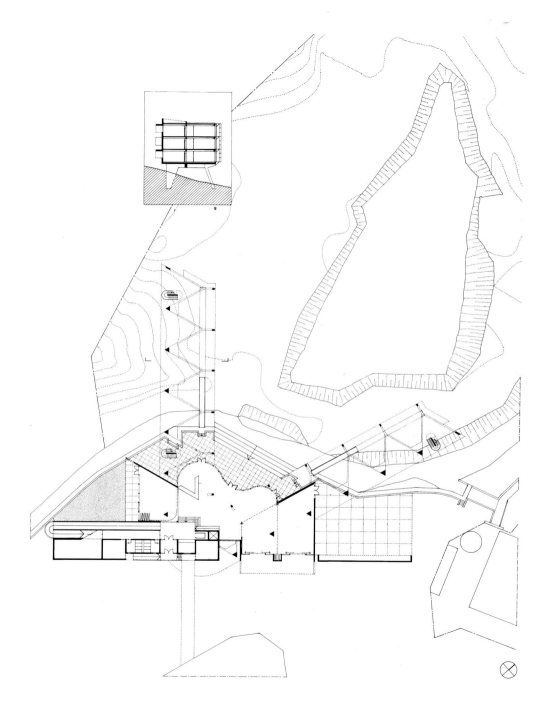

Client: Sto AG. **Accommodation**: Offices for the expansion of all departments, training and meeting rooms, exhibition and multi-purpose space. **Schedule of net areas m²**, total: 5,470, Offices 2,470, Meeting spaces 600, Exhibition 130, Multi-purpose space 600, Ancillary 780, Circulation 720, Plant 170. **Architect**: Michael Wilford and Partners, London and Stuttgart. Manfred Klemt, Karin Ludewig, Stuart McKnight, Ian McMillan, Manuel Schupp, Charlie Sutherland, Karen Waloschek, Simon Whiting. **Consultants**: Structural Engineers: Boll & Partner, Stuttgart. Mechanical Engineers: Jaeger, Mornhinweg & Partner, Stuttgart. Electrical Engineers: Ingenieurbüro für Elektrotechnik Schwarz, GmbH, Stuttgart.

STO OFFICE & TRAINING WEIZEN

This office building with staff training facilities and associated meeting rooms forms part of the fifteen year redevelopment plan for the headquarters and manufacturing plant. The building comprises two primary elements: a pair of spreading office wings embracing the lake, located above a cluster of free-form ground-level training spaces, situated beneath the junction of the wings.

Three office floors are elevated on zig zag columns, allowing the undulating landscape and meandering river to flow beneath the building. Individual offices are ranged along either side of a central corridor in each wing and are connected by a flexible meeting room and central reception area. Saw-toothed glazing to the meeting rooms provides diagonal valley views.

Training spaces define the factory truck yard and screen it from the valley. A cafe opens onto a riverside terrace with views across the lake, framed by the office wings above. The lift shaft pins both elements of the building together and a bridge over the truck yard connects the building to the main entrance of the headquarters as an extension of a major north/south pedestrian axis.

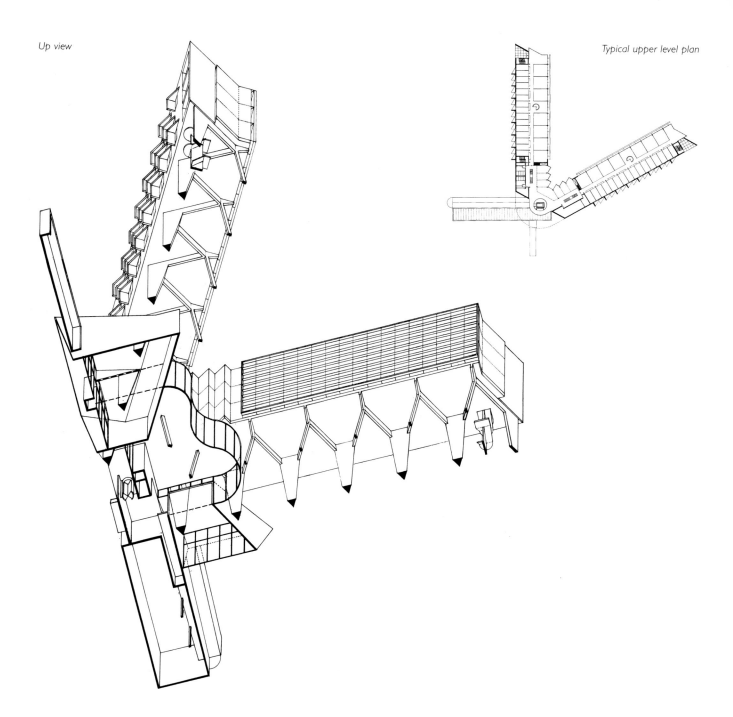

Up view

Typical upper level plan

*Down view of
training facilities*

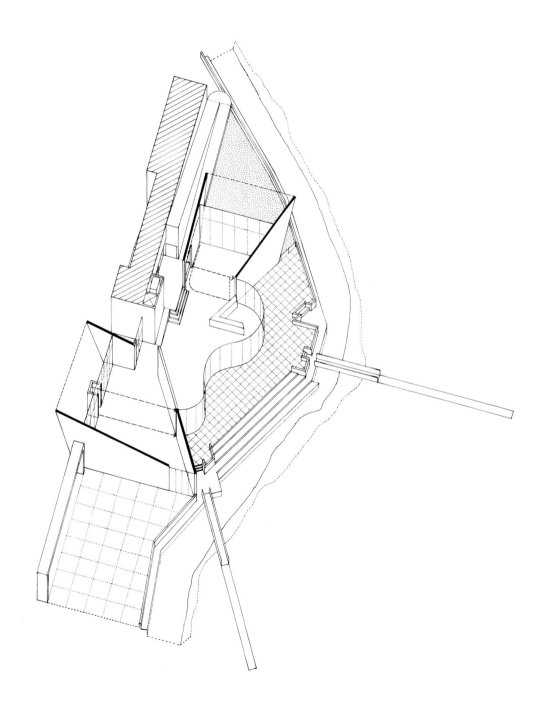

STO COMMUNICATIONS WEIZEN

1994

This is the first of the new buildings planned on the valley edge of the company's Headquarters. It comprises three elements; marketing offices, an oval entrance pavilion and a square base containing training facilities. The building nestles between existing structures, connected by a footbridge to the first phase of the raised central garden.

The office wing glides above the training building, facing the primary approach and forming a dramatic gateway. Its elegant structure heightens the floating sensation and minimises obstruction of views of the valley from the central garden. Offices with spectacular views across the surrounding landscape are arranged on four floors along the outer edges of the tapered plan, enclosing a central lift, stairs, and service cores. Each office floor has a slipped relationship with the one below providing a dynamic silhouette, and stepped balconies reconcile the scale difference between the new and existing buildings.

The oval entrance pavilion is connected by lift and stairs to the marketing offices above and training facilities below. For outdoor social functions the lounge area opens onto a large terrace above the training facilities. Seminar rooms and an exhibition area are situated at ground floor level, with flexible partitions to allow various spatial arrangements for receptions and staff gatherings. A separate lower entrance will accommodate lectures, meetings and social events outside office hours.

The practical training areas, in which people are taught how to use the company's products, form the lowest floor of the building and open out to an adjacent external work area. Screen walls extend into the landscape from opposite corners of the training building, to provide outdoor exhibition space for the company's products.

The office wing is of reinforced concrete construction, surfaced externally with white painted insulated stucco. Curved blue metal panels enclose the opaque section of the oval pavilion. The walls and terrace of the training square are clad with diagonally set panels of dark grey basalt stone, the voids of which are filled with coloured enamel. Inside, the pleated concrete structure of the oval pavilion will be painted to match the exterior. The elevator shaft and stair tower will be finished in turquoise and orange stucco.

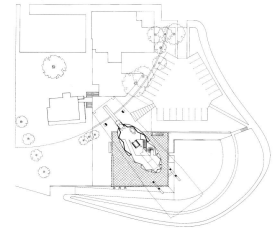

Garden level plan

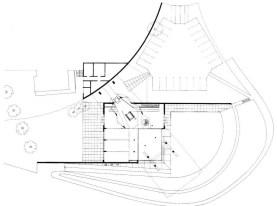

Training level plan

Client: Sto AG. **Accommodation**: Offices for the marketing department, multi-purpose seminar and exhibition spaces with practical training workshops. **Schedule of net areas m²,** total: 5,170, Offices 1,390, Meeting rooms120, Exhibition 280, Theoretical training 150, Practical training 200, Ancillary 550, Circulation 970, Plant 270, Terrace 1,240. **Architects**: Michael Wilford and Partners, London and Stuttgart, Jürgen Engelhardt, Irmgard Gassner, Daphne Kephalidis, Heike Lentz, Karin Ludewig, Markus Mangold, Stuart McKnight, Ian McMillan, Manuel Schupp, Daniel Seibert, Andy Strickland, Charlie Sutherland, Richard Walker, Karen Waloschek. **Consultants**: Structural Engineers: Boll & Partner, Stuttgart. Mechanical Engineers: Jaeger, Mornhinweg & Partner, Stuttgart. Electrical Engineers: Ingenierubüro für Elektrotechnik Schwarz , GmbH, Stuttgart. Building physicist: Dr. Schäcke und Bayer.

Opposite – Shadow site plan showing position of Building K

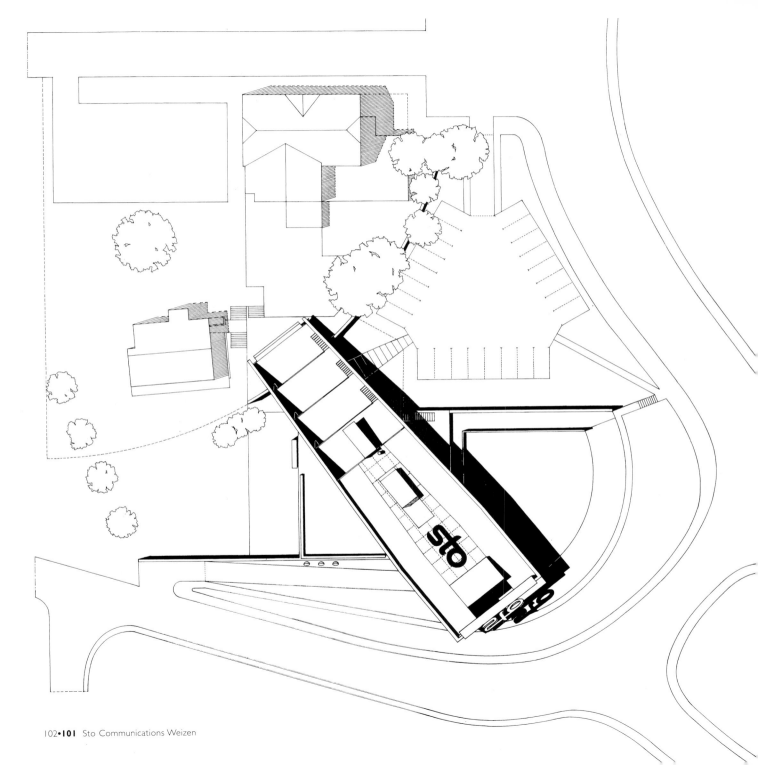

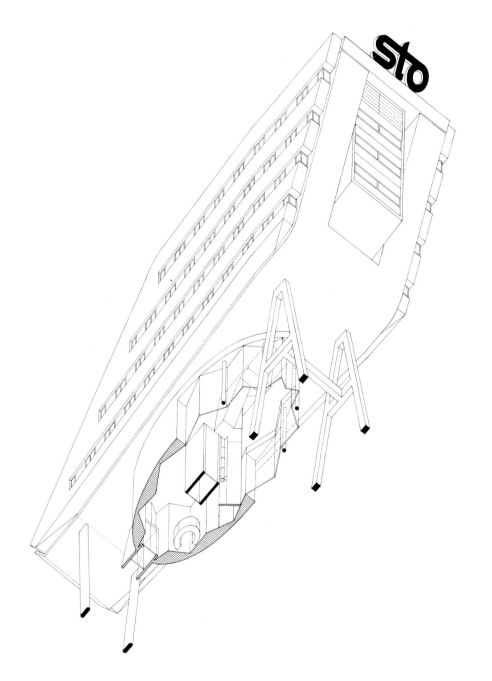

Sectional up view

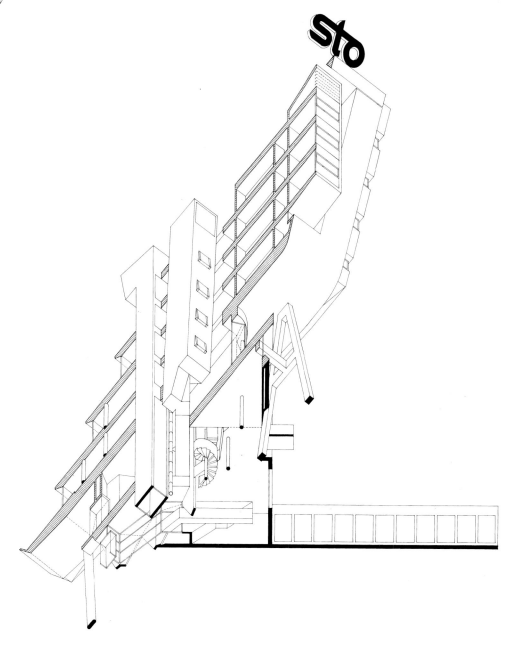

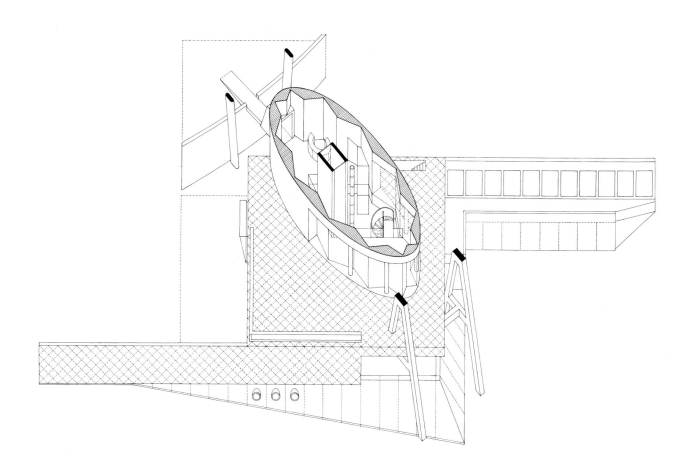

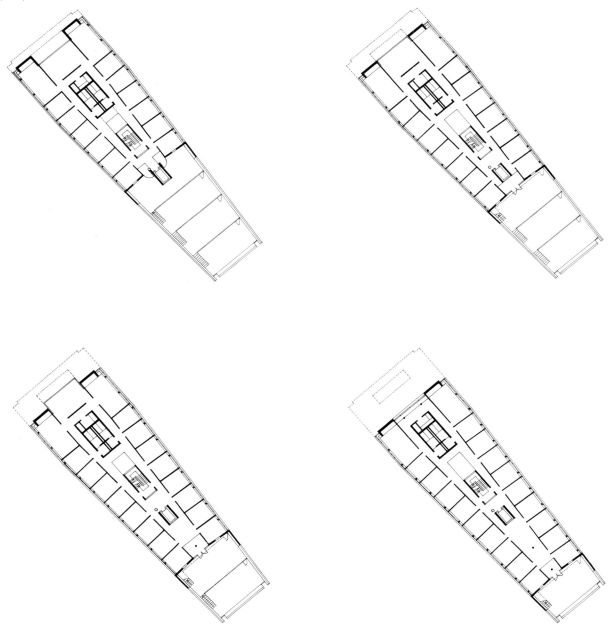

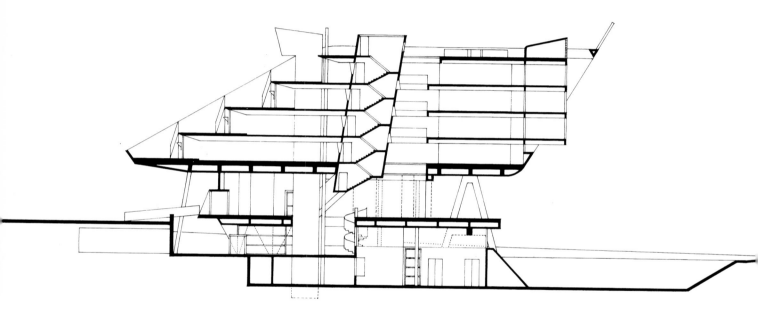

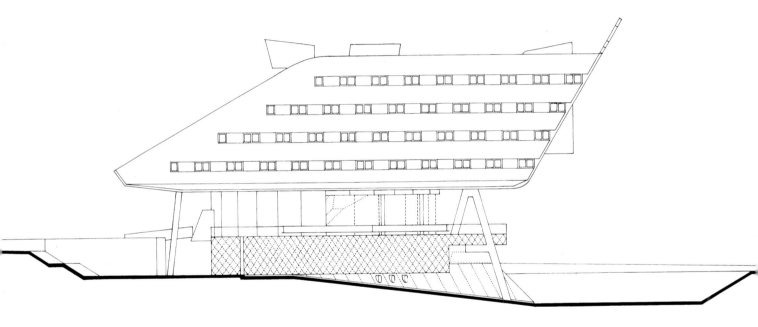

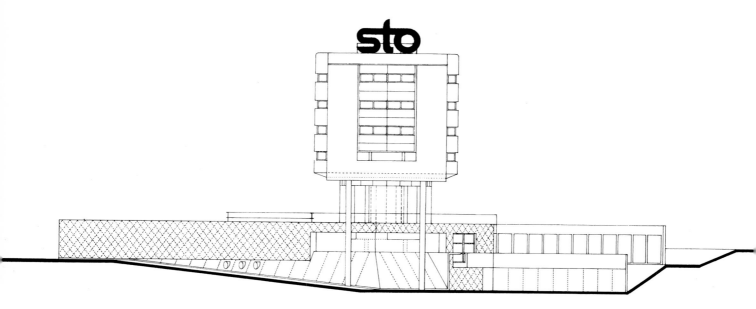

Garden elevation

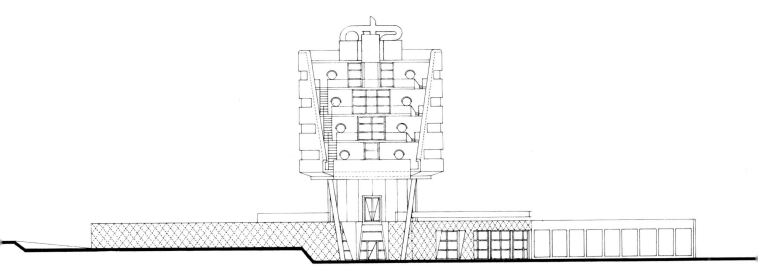

STO DEPOT HAMBURG

1994–1995

This project is a prototype for a series of regional depots to be constructed throughout Germany for local distribution of the company's products. Each depot will comprise four building elements – warehousing, offices for the regional sales force, an exhibition area and a customer training pavilion. Modular forms and envelopes have been designed for each of these elements, which are capable of assembly in a variety of combinations to suit different site configurations.

The Hamburg depot is located on a corner site in a light industrial park on the fringe of the city. The building elements are oriented in three directions. The warehouse is at right angles to the geometry of surrounding buildings and parallel to the primary street frontage. The offices are set diagonally across the corner of the site and the training pavilion faces the entrance to the site. A curving display wall beneath the offices encloses the exhibition area and secluded garden.

The main elements combine to enclose a central operations counter at entry level and private outdoor staff courtyard above. The warehouse street facade is elaborated to form a public face to the building with a full length canopy, and the tower sign registers the building in its largely featureless context.

Customers may place urgent orders at the 'drive up' window adjacent to the entrance or less urgent requirements at the operations counter inside. Upper level offices are ranged along a central corridor with the branch manager overlooking the forecourt. The curved roof of the office building contains an unfinished loft to provide for future expansion.

Each building element is steel-framed with the offices elevated on a concrete 'table'. External walls comprise unique factory-made lightweight cladding panels, developed from low cost materials for a wide range of applications in office, industrial and residential buildings.

The external colour scheme incorporates Sto's

corporate identity on the street facade of the warehouse and tower. The offices, training building and end facade of the warehouse are painted in primary colours to enhance their individuality and to communicate Sto's business interest in colour. Inside, the segmental ceiling of the exhibition space is decorated in pastel shades of spectrum colours.

The design is an extrovert expression of each functional element through contrasting architectural form and colour to provide a stimulating and attractive place for customers and staff.

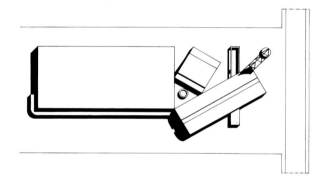

Client: Sto AG. **Accommodation**: Warehouse, offices, exhibition and training areas. **Schedule of net areas m²**, total: 2,630, Offices 300, Training Areas 230, Exhibition Space 380, Warehouse 1,480, External Insulation Store 240. **Architects**: Michael Wilford & Partners, London and Stuttgart, Kenneth Beattie, Jurgen Engelhardt, Karin Ludewig, Markus Mangold, Ian McMillan, Stuart McKnight, Manuel Schupp, Jutta Simpfendörfer, Charlie Sutherland, Karen Waloschek. **Consultants**: Structural Engineers: Boll & Partner, Stuttgart. Mechanical Engineers: Jaeger, Mornhinweg & Partner, Stuttgart. Cost Consultant: Davis Langdon & Weiss GmbH, Stuttgart. Supervising Architect: Rüdiger Franke, Hamburg. Electrical Engineers: Ingenieurbüro für Elektrotechnik Schwarz GmbH, Stuttgart. Building physicist: Dr. Schäcke und Bayer.

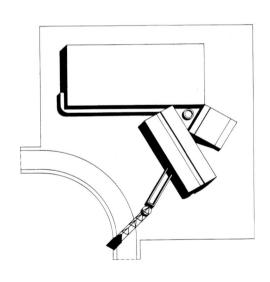

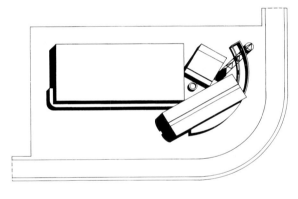

Alternative depot
arrangements

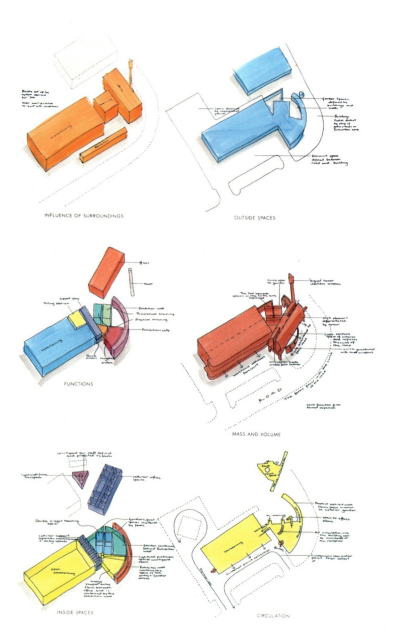

INFLUENCE OF SURROUNDINGS

OUTSIDE SPACES

FUNCTIONS

MASS AND VOLUME

INSIDE SPACES

CIRCULATION

Cross section

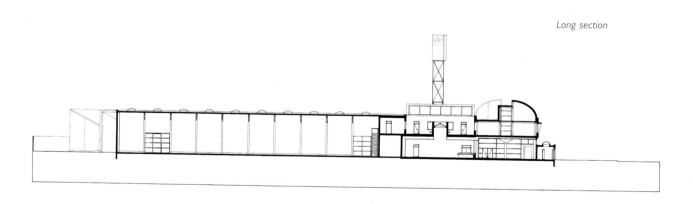

Long section

Upper level plan

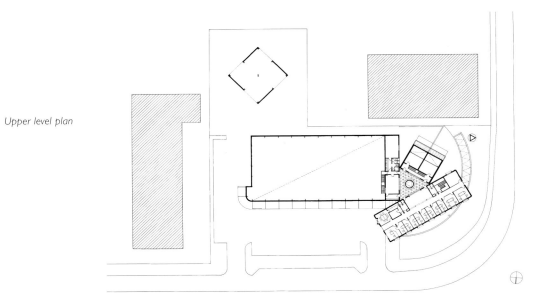

Ground level plan

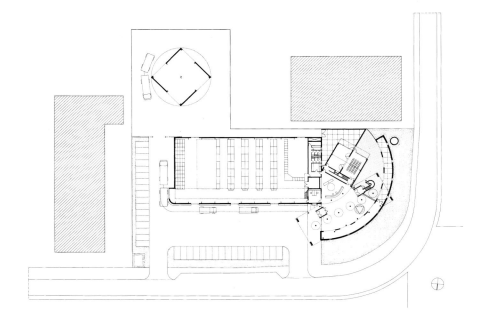

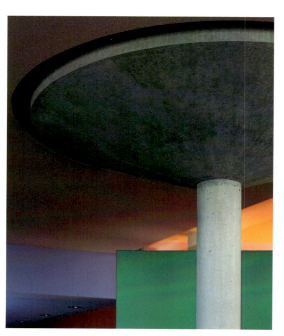

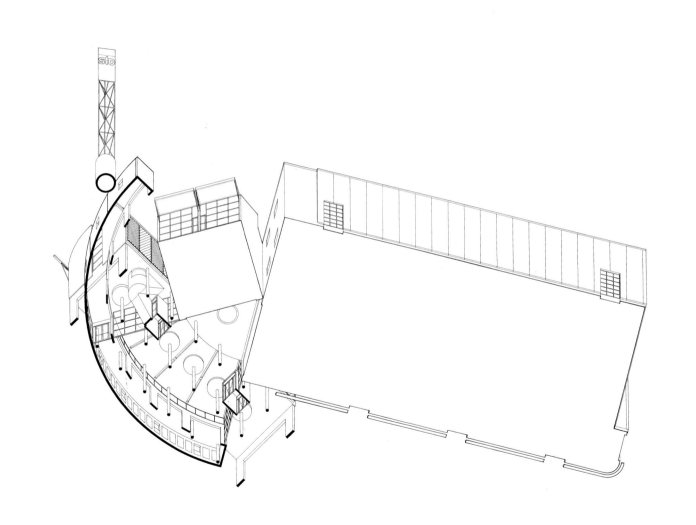

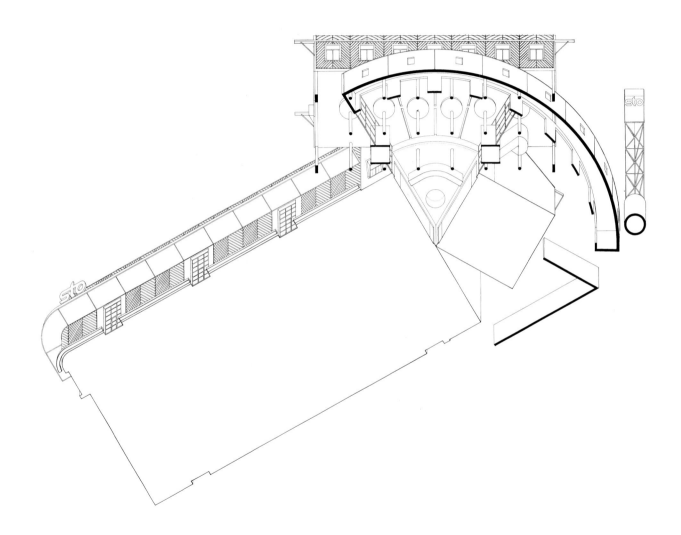

THE BRITISH EMBASSY

BRITISH EMBASSY BERLIN

1995—

The British Embassy will re-occupy its central location on Wilhelmstrasse when Berlin becomes the Federal Capital of Germany. The nearby Berlin Wall sterilised the immediate area for 30 years, and only now is there the opportunity for the district to regain something of its earlier 20th Century pre-eminence.

Lined with grand palais, Wilhelmstrasse formed the western edge of the 18th Century expansion of the medieval city. Further development in the 19th Century and early 20th Century transformed Wilhelmstrasse into a city centre street and due to their close proximity to the Reichstag many of the palais became government ministries . Most buildings lining Wilhelmstrasse were destroyed in World War II and the area between the Tiergarten and Wilhelmstrasse became a wide, open swathe through the urban fabric, associated with the Wall.

The generous Embassy site allows the provision of open spaces within the city block, similar to the courtyards of the pre-war Palais and allowing daylight and natural ventilation into the heart of the Embassy.

A combined vehicle and pedestrian Gateway from Wilhelmstrasse leads to the Entrance Court providing an elegant approach and set-down within the building. The Court is a transition in ambience and culture between the City and Embassy. An oak tree at its centre will provide an immediate association with Britain.

On ceremonial occasions visitors will be formally received and escorted up the grand staircase to the Wintergarden on the 'piano nobile' level above. Bathed in sunshine from circular rooflights and with generous windows overlooking the entrance court, the Wintergarden is the internal focus of the Embassy.

The Consulate is accessed from the gateway, and staff enter and leave the building through the Entrance Hall via a security door adjacent to the lift core. Everyone visiting and working in the Embassy is, therefore, able to experience the dignity and grandeur of the interior. A circular Conference Room and formal Dining Room overlooking Wilhelmstrasse are arranged around the Wintergarden so that they may be used individually or together for grand banquets and large exhibitions.

Offices and staff circulation balconies encircle upper levels of the Wintergarden offering visitors glimpses of activities in the building above and staff views of special events on the 'piano nobile' below.

The street facade establishes a 22 metre high stone plane across the full width of the site, as required by the city urban development guidelines. This plane is an expression of the layered internal organisation of the building comprising base, ceremonial level and offices. An abstract collage of forms is revealed through an opening in the facade, marking the entrance and registering the special character of the Embassy in relation to the neutrality of adjacent buildings. They hint at the special spaces contained within the Embassy and encourage the visitor's sense of curiosity and anticipation.

The new British Embassy will have a modern dignified personality whilst respecting the City's tradition of building massing, articulation and materials.

Opposite – context plan

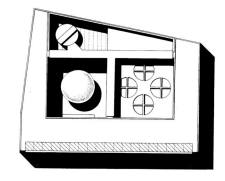

Shadow plan

Opposite – Elevation showing Embassy and Brandenburg Gate

Client: Overseas Estates Department, Foreign & Commonwealth Office, Whitehall. **Accommodation**: Embassy and Diplomatic facilities. **Schedule of gross areas m²**, total: 8,910, Offices 3,549, Staff offices 265, Conference 222, Dining 45, Winter garden 614, Ancillary 609, Circulation 2,102, Car park 492, Plant 1,012. **Architects**: Michael Wilford and Partners, Paul Barke, Iain Clavadetscher, Robert Dinse, Stuart McKnight, Gillan McInnes, David Reat, Leandro Rotondi, Sven Schmedes, Manuel Schupp, Charlie Sutherland, Simon Usher, Karen Waloschek, Ulrike Wilke. **Consultants**: Project Manager: Schal International, London. Structural, Mechanical and Electrical Engineers: Whitby & Bird, London, with Boll und Partner, Stuttgart and Jaeger, Mornhinweg and Partner, Stuttgart. Electrical Engineer: Ingenieurbüro für Elektrotechnik Schwarz, GmbH, Stuttgart. Quantity Surveyor: Hanscomb, London. Building Physicist: Dr.Flohrer, Berlin. Fire Consultant: Hosser Hass & Partner, Berling-Grunewald.

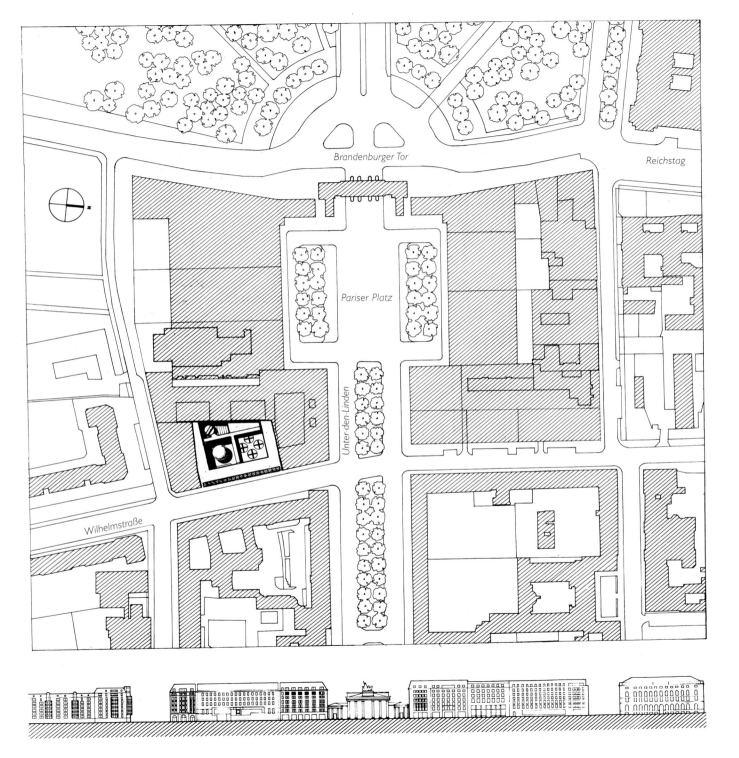

Brandenburger Tor

Reichstag

Pariser Platz

Unter den Linden

Wilhelmstraße

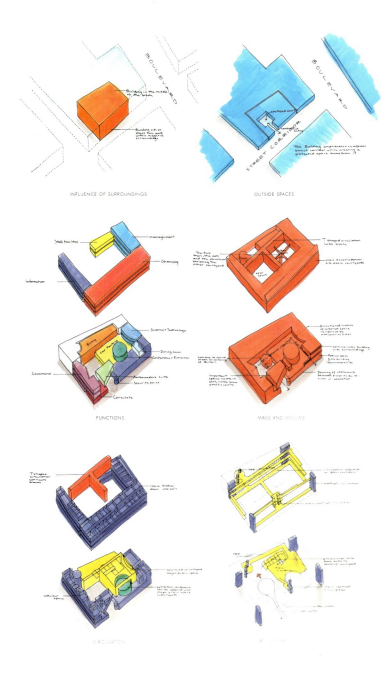

INFLUENCE OF SURROUNDINGS

OUTSIDE SPACES

FUNCTIONS

MASS AND VOLUME

CIRCULATION

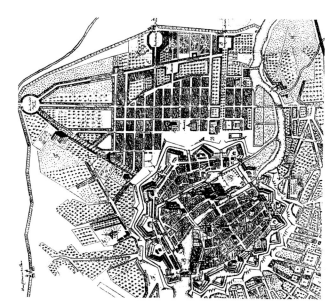

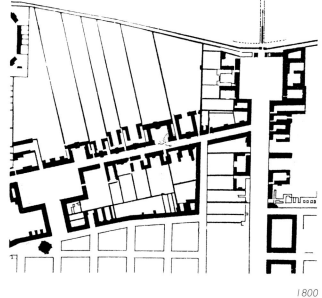

Historic maps of Berlin and Wilhelmstraße　　　　　　　　　　　　　*1737*

　　　　　　　　　　　　　　　　　　　　　　　　　　　　　　　　1800

　　　　　　　　　　　　　　　　1936　　　　　　　　　　　　　　　　*1988*

Wilhelmstraße looking north, 1934

Wilhelmstraße, looking south 1991

Schinkel Building on Unter den Linden (destroyed)

Adlon Hotel (destroyed)

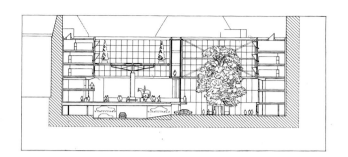

Long section

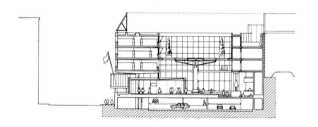

*Cross section through
wintergarden*

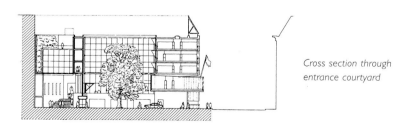

*Cross section through
entrance courtyard*

Upper level plan

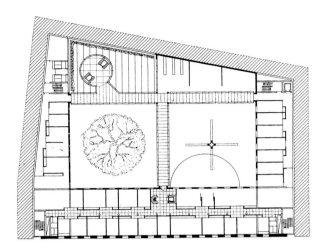

First floor plan

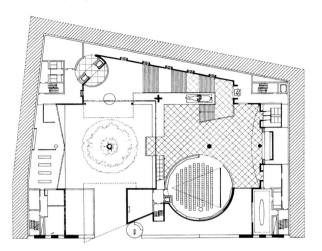

Second floor plan

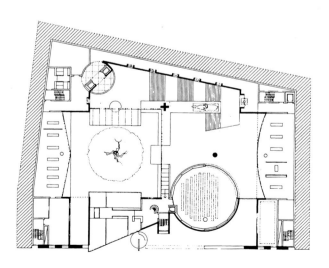

Ground floor plan

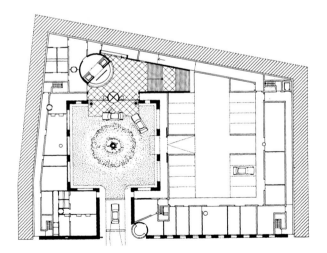

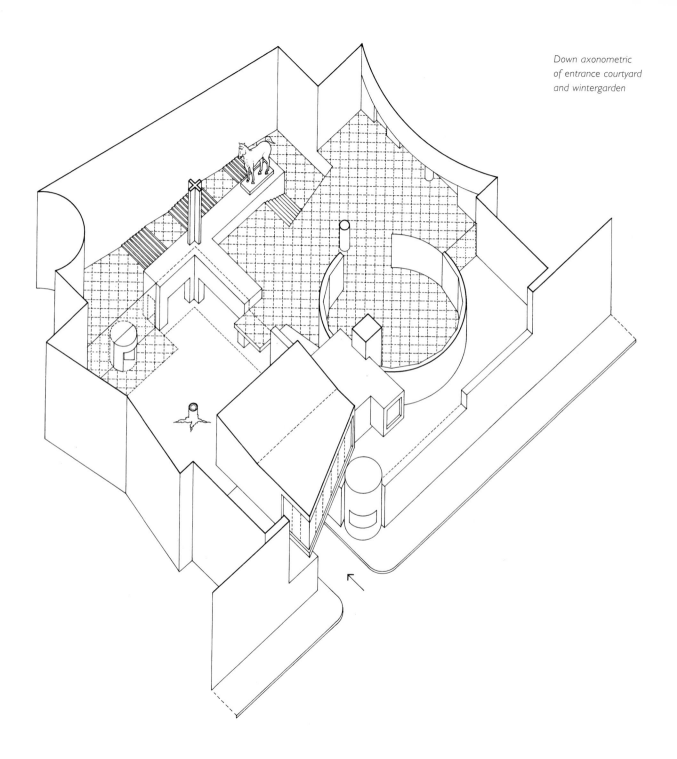

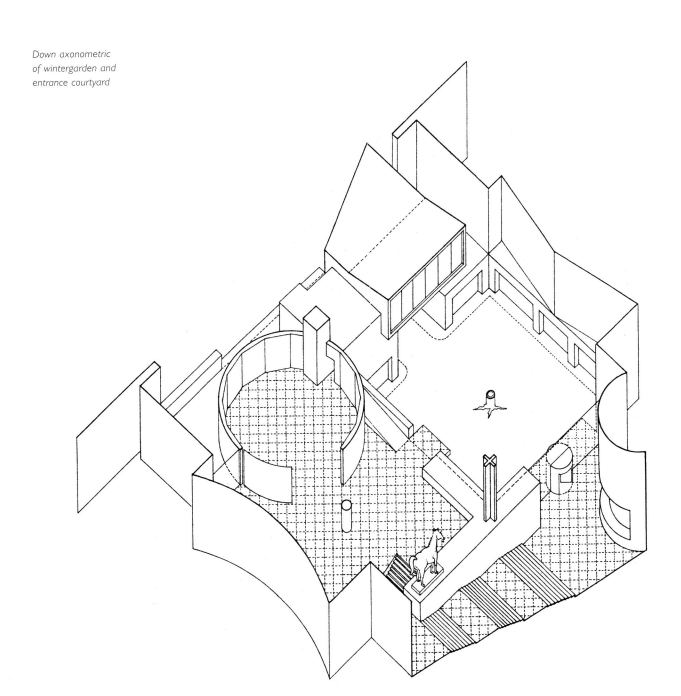

Down axonometric of wintergarden and entrance courtyard

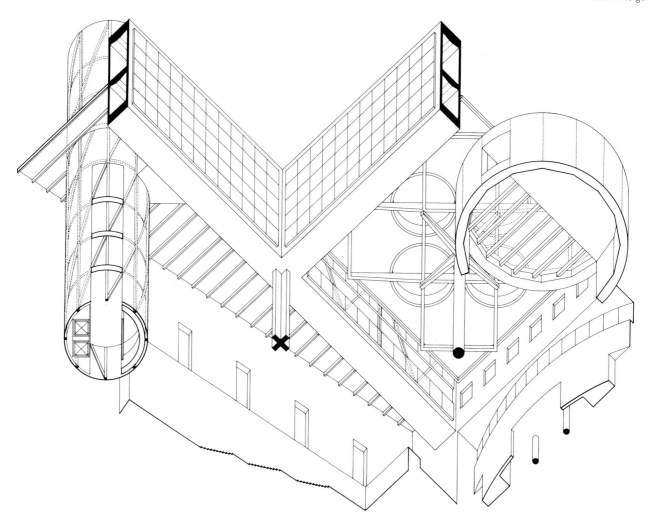

Up axonometric of entrance courtyard and wintergarden

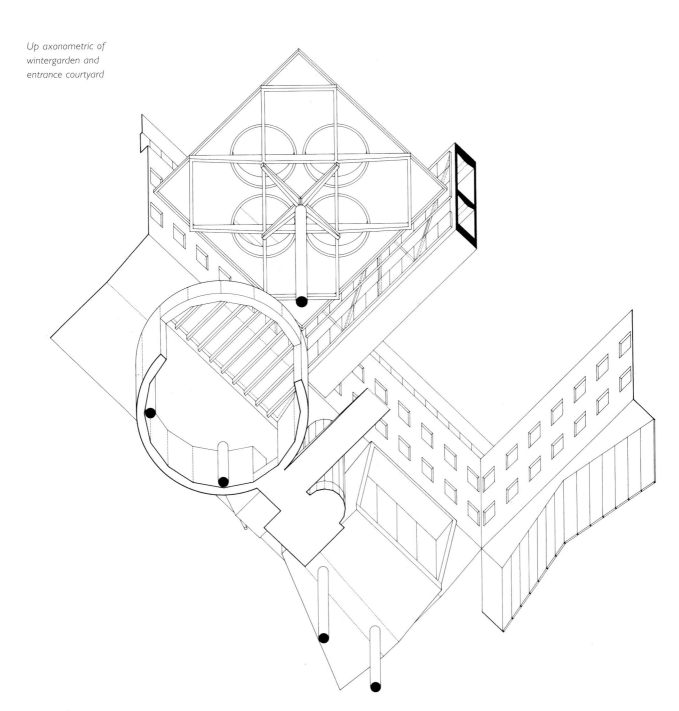

Up axonometric of wintergarden and entrance courtyard

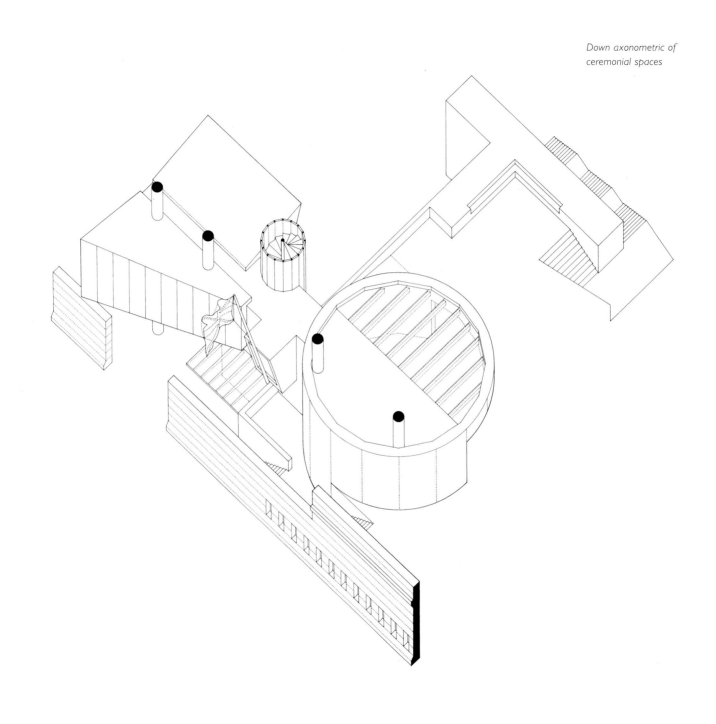

*Down axonometric of
ceremonial spaces*

Down axonometric of
ceremonial spaces .

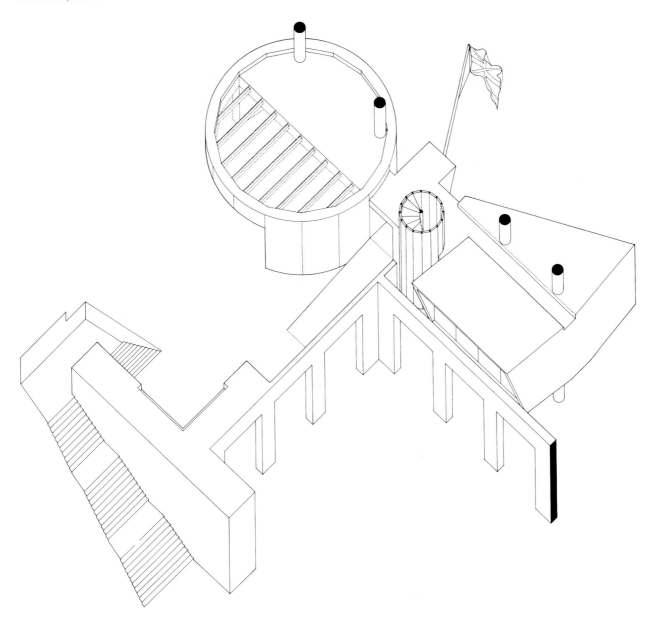

LOWRY CENTRE SALFORD

1992 –

The Lowry Centre will accommodate facilities for both visual and performing arts to provide an exciting, stimulating venue for recreation and education. Bordered by the Manchester Ship Canal and facing a new triangular public Plaza, it will be the landmark focus of the redevelopment of Salford Quays. The Plaza will be a sheltered and lively venue for community activity, gathering together three primary approaches to the Centre, including the terminus of the new Metrolink, light rapid transit system. An hotel and parking building, enclose the remaining sides and waterside promenades provide leisurely pedestrian routes from the entrance to the Quays.

The building contains a 1650 seat Lyric Theatre, a 400 seat Flexible Theatre with rehearsal and dressing facilities, Art Galleries to display the City's collection of L. S. Lowry paintings as well as changing exhibitions, a Children's Gallery, together with bars, cafe and waterfront restaurant.

A grand two storey high foyer, open throughout the day, extends across the full width of the Plaza frontage to provide clear and convenient access to all activities. The Lyric Theatre forms the heart of the building with stairs and balconies providing direct access to three auditorium seating levels. Pavilions on either side of the foyer accommodate entrances to the Children's Gallery and Lowry Galleries above. Shops and box office adjacent to the entrance can be entered either from the Plaza or foyer.

The Adaptable Theatre, on an axis aligned with the Lyric Theatre, has a courtyard form to suit various performance arrangements and a curved enclosing foyer with dramatic views across the ship canal. An internal promenade around the building enables visitors to browse and enjoy all activities throughout the day. The Lowry Centre Galleries provide a flexible suite of rooms of varying scale and ambience with loggias for relaxation and views out of the building. The Children's

Gallery comprises a dramatic, stepped linear volume containing a series of geometric forms to accommodate interactive exhibits and audio-visual displays.

The bar, cafe and restaurant are ranged along the southern side of the building. In fine weather, the facilities can be extended onto quayside terraces overlooking the canal turning basin. Upper level bars on either side of the Lyric Theatre open on to roof terraces above the foyer with views across the plaza.

As the workplace of a wide variety of people, the layout of the building will encourage a sense of artistic community. Rehearsal spaces are provided adjacent to the Lyric Theatre and above the Adaptable Theatre, with the artists' lounge and roof garden located over the central scenery store. The administration tower is crowned by an illuminated sign announcing current productions and registering the presence of the Lowry Centre on the Salford skyline.

Site

Client: Lowry Centre trustees and City of Salford. **Accomodation**: Galleries for the City of Salford's Lowry Collection, Lowry Study Centre, Children's Galleries 1,650 Seat Lyric theatre, 400 seat flexible theatre, rehearsal and dressing room facilities, bars, cafe and retail. **Schedule of gross areas m²**, total: 23,930, Lyric Theatre (1,650) 3,070, Adaptable Theatre (450 seats) 1,630, Front of House 6,230, Back of House 6,345, Lowry Galleries 1,410, Children's Galleries 1,120, Administration Offices 1,560, Catering/Hospitality 1,330, Plant 1,235, **Architect**: Michael Wilford and Partners, Paul Barke, Liam Hennessy, David Jennings, Chris Matthews, Gillian McInnes, Stuart McKnight, Alison McLellan, Ian McMillan, Adele Pascal, Andrew Pryke, Charlie Sutherland, Joanna Sutherland, Karen Waloschek. **Consultants**: Architects: Michael Wilford and Partners Ltd. Theatre Consultant: Theatre Projects Consultants. Museum Consultant: Lord Cultural Resources. Acoustics: Sandy Brown Associates. Quantity Surveyors: Davis Langdon & Everest and Bucknall Austin. Structural, Mechanical and Electrical Engineers: Buro Happold. Project Manager: Gleeds Management Services.

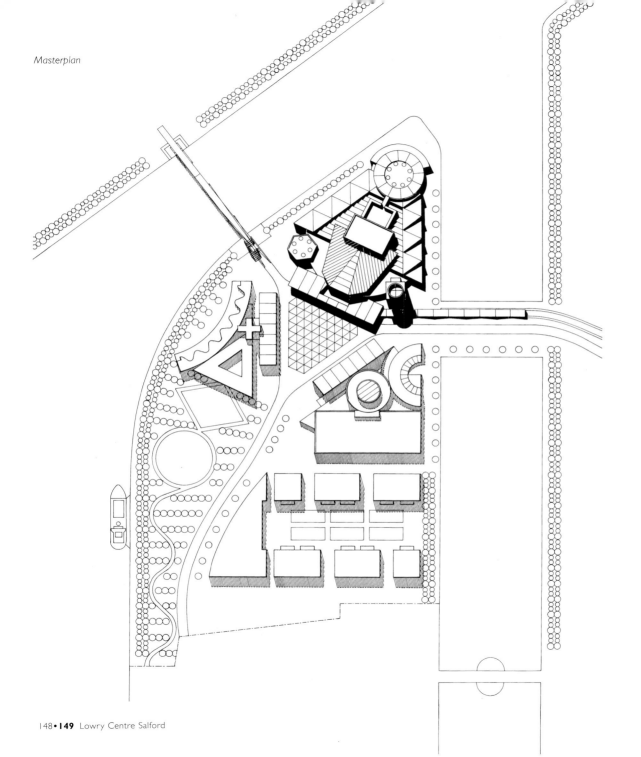

Masterplan

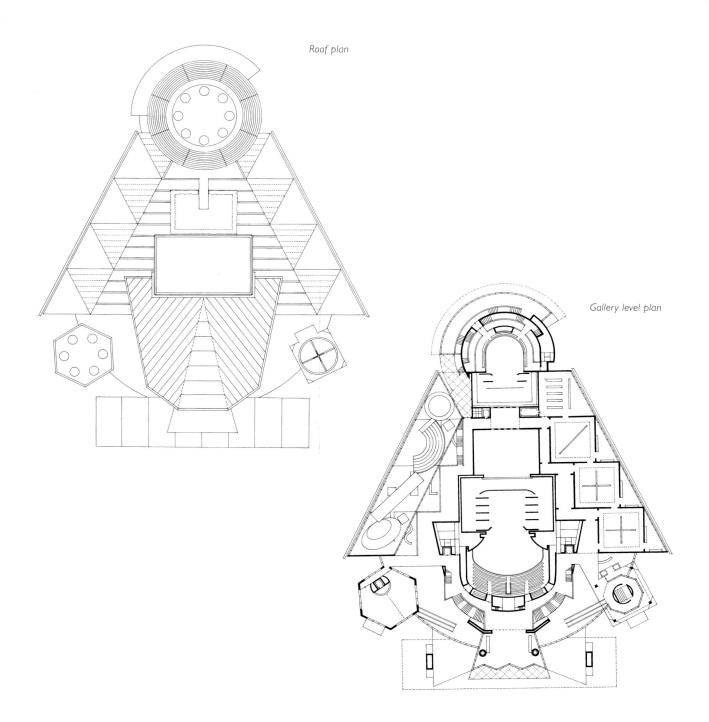

Roof plan

Gallery level plan

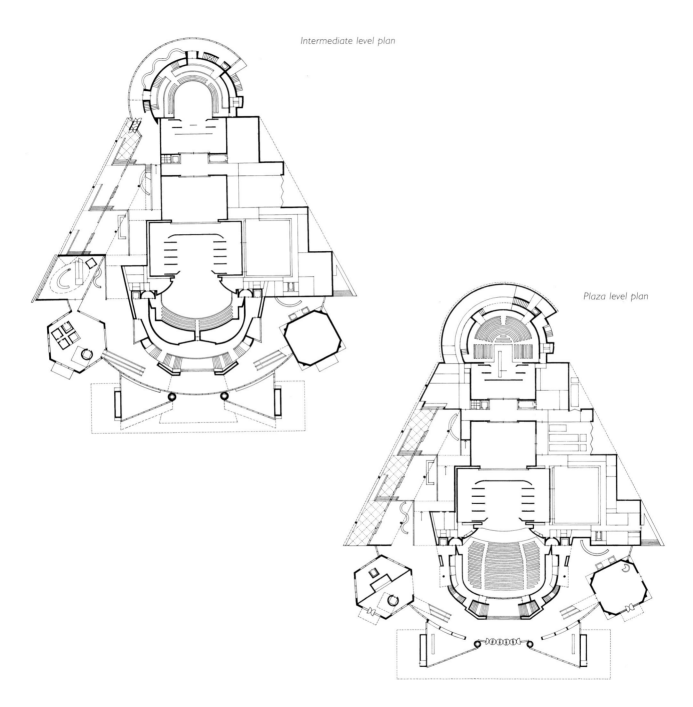

Intermediate level plan

Plaza level plan

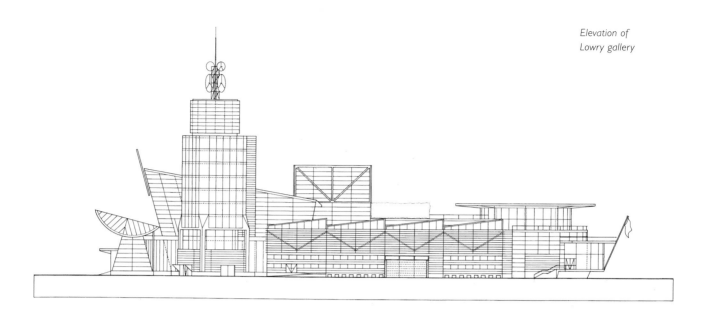

Elevation of
Lowry gallery

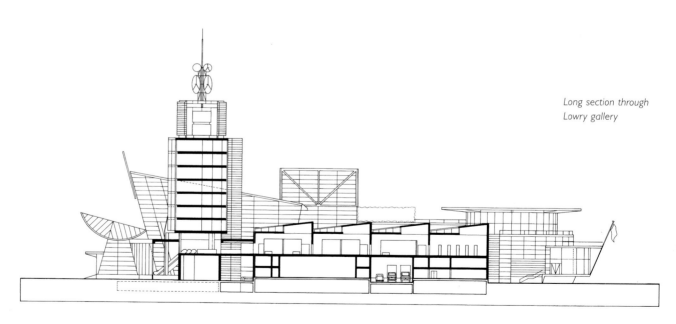

Long section through
Lowry gallery

*Elevation of
children's gallery*

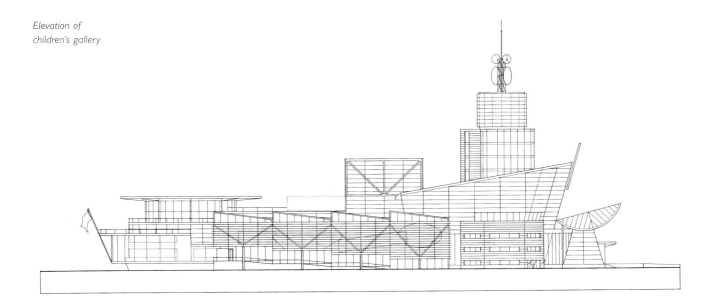

*Long section through
children's gallery*

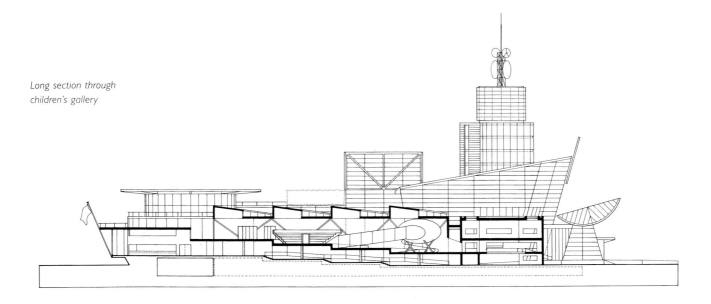

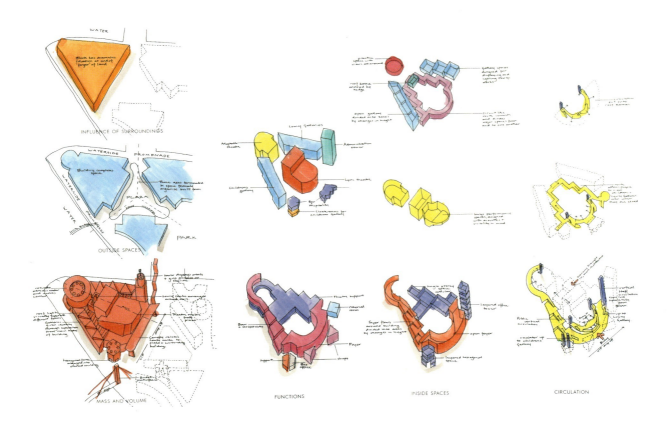

INFLUENCE OF SURROUNDINGS

OUTSIDE SPACES

MASS AND VOLUME

FUNCTIONS

INSIDE SPACES

CIRCULATION

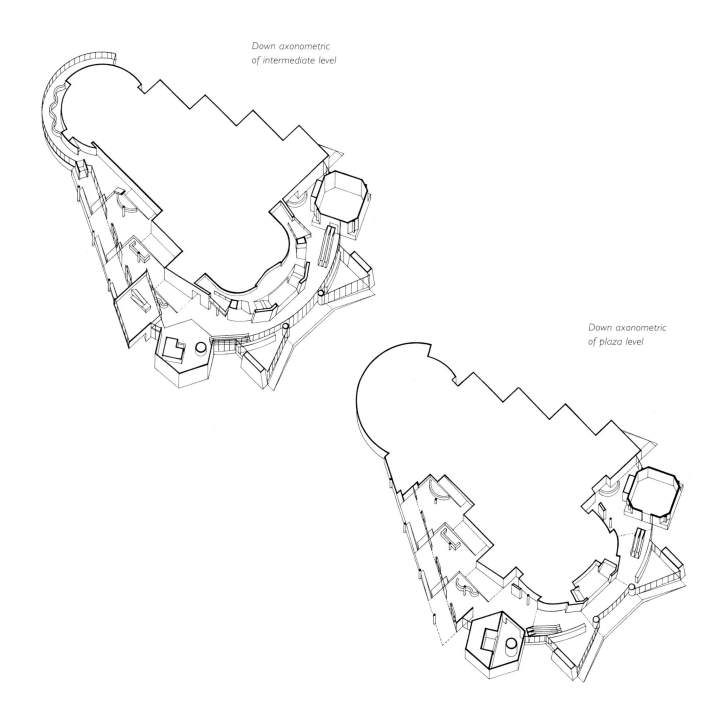

*Down axonometric
of intermediate level*

*Down axonometric
of plaza level*

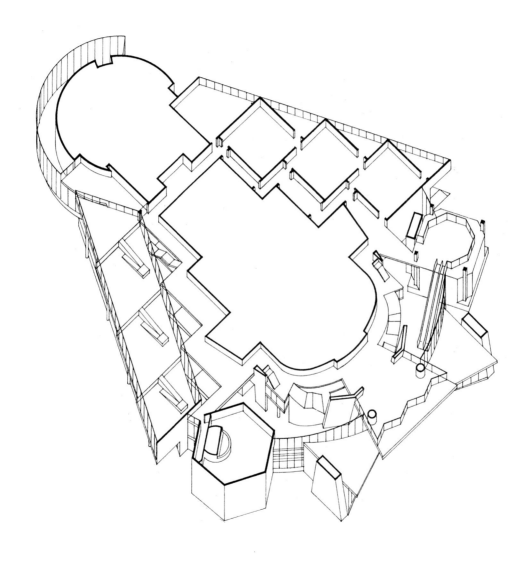

SCIENCE LIBARY U.C. IRVINE CALIFORNIA

1988–1994

The campus has a 'wheel' plan, with a circular park at the hub and linear academic quadrangles radiating from it into the surrounding landscape. The outer edge of the park is defined by a circular pedestrian promenade linking the quadrangles. Parking and service areas are accessed from an outer ring road. The Biological Sciences quadrangle on which the library is situated, also connects the Medical School to the centre of the campus.

The library is a campus landmark, visible from all approaches and centrepiece of the Bio Sci Quad. Its unique form responds to the brief which required a coherent organisation, direct connections between departments, and daylight to all reader and staff spaces. Limited site area between an existing single storey building and the quad axis determined the narrow library entrance portal facing the promenade.

The courtyard enables the entrance to be located at the heart of the building and provides daylight to

the interior. The buildings architectural composition allows it to face equally in opposite directions and to define an entrance to the Bio Sci quad from the centre of the campus. Internally, it provides direct functional connections and flexibility of use whilst avoiding a 'warehouse' solution.

The entrance portal is the first of a sequence of contracting and expanding spaces created by the building to encourage entry and passage beneath it. The circular courtyard is a cool, shaded outdoor space, and visible activity in the library enlivens the route to the medical school.

The accommodation is arranged on five floors. Entry is from the courtyard via a dramatic stair to the loan desk on level 2. Reference and periodical libraries are combined in a double height reading room encircling the courtyard to provide flexibility in layout and convenient movement from one section to another.

On levels 3, 4, and 5 stack areas parallel to the

triangular sides of the upper courtyard, accommodate bound periodicals with monographs in the long wing. A variety of reader spaces are distributed throughout the building, offering a choice of location from centres of high activity to absolute seclusion. Double height reading rooms terminate the extremities of the building and study carrels line the outer wall of the central drum.

Three central lifts and five staircases distributed across the plan provide convenient vertical circulation between all facilities.

The building is of steel framed construction with steel studded exterior walls surfaced with coloured stucco, delineated by a red sandstone base and string course to express the layered organisation of the building. The courtyard is also surfaced with red sandstone.

Opposite – Context plan

University of California at Irvine campus

Client: University of California, Irvine. **Accommodation**: Bookstack and reader areas, study rooms, reference and periodicals library, public and technical services departments, learning resources centre, computer suite and staff facilities. **Schedule of net areas m²**, total: 16150, Bookstack Areas (2,000 modules) 3680, Reader Space (1,625 spaces)3300, Study Rooms 550, Reference and Periodicals Section (350 modules + spaces) 330 1700, Public Services 520, Technical Services 1250, Learning Resources (170 spaces) 420, Computer Suite 110, Staff Facilities 130, Ancillary, Support Facilities and Circulation 3950. **Client**: James Stirling Michael Wilford and Associates, Chris Chong, Felim Dunne, Eilis O'Donnell, Richard Portchmouth, Peter Ray, Mike Russum. **Consultants**: Associate Architects: IBI/L Paul Zajfen, California. Mechanical/Electrical Engineers: Ove Arup and Partners London/California. Structural Engineers: Ove Arup and Partners London/California. Cost Consultant: Adamson Associates, California. Landscape: Burton & Spitz, California.

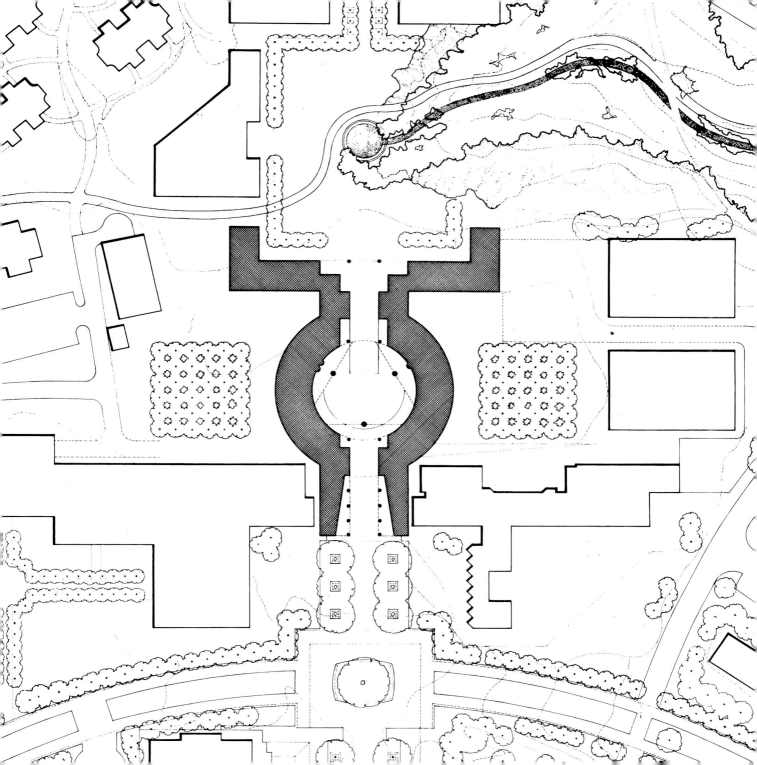

INFLUENCE OF SURROUNDINGS

OUTSIDE SPACES

MASS AND VOLUME

FUNCTIONS

INSIDE SPACES

CIRCULATION

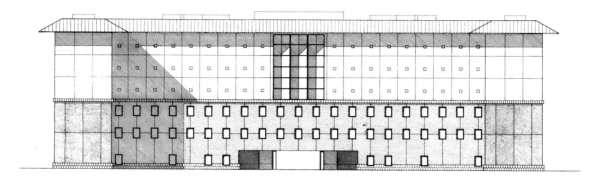

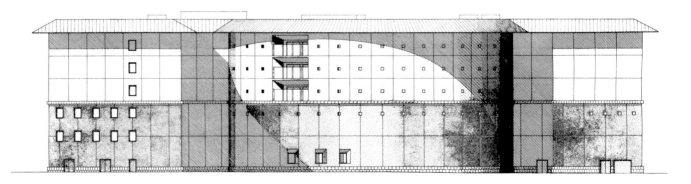

Cross section through courtyard

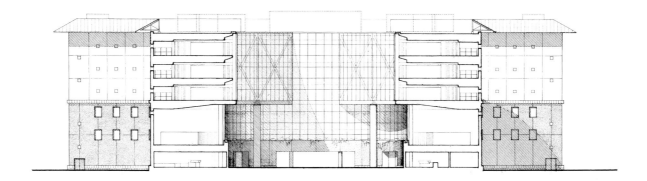

*Long section through
courtyard and public walkway*

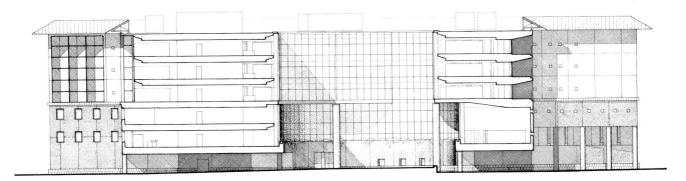

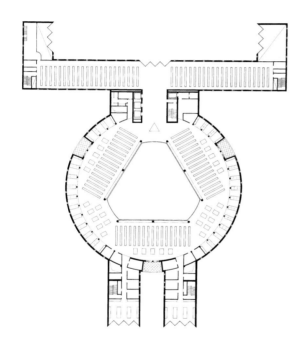

Typical upper level plan

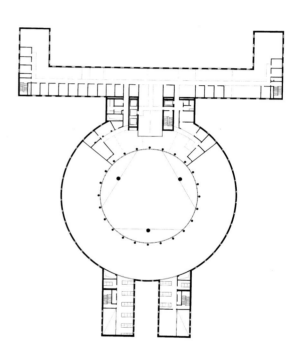

Mezzanine level plan

Reference and
periodicals library plan

Entrance level plan

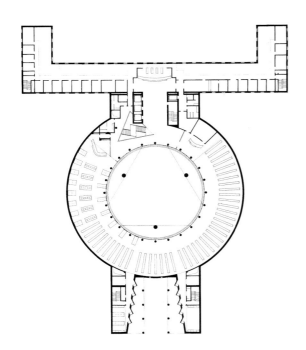
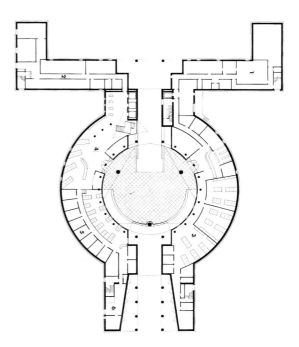

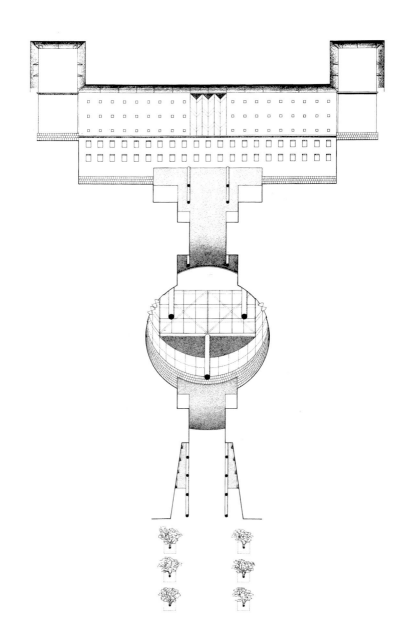

*Up view showing
public walkway
from square to
centre of campus*

*Up view showing
public walkway
from centre of
campus to square*

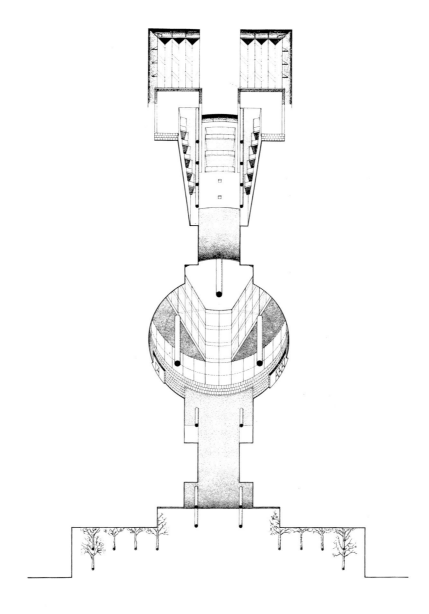

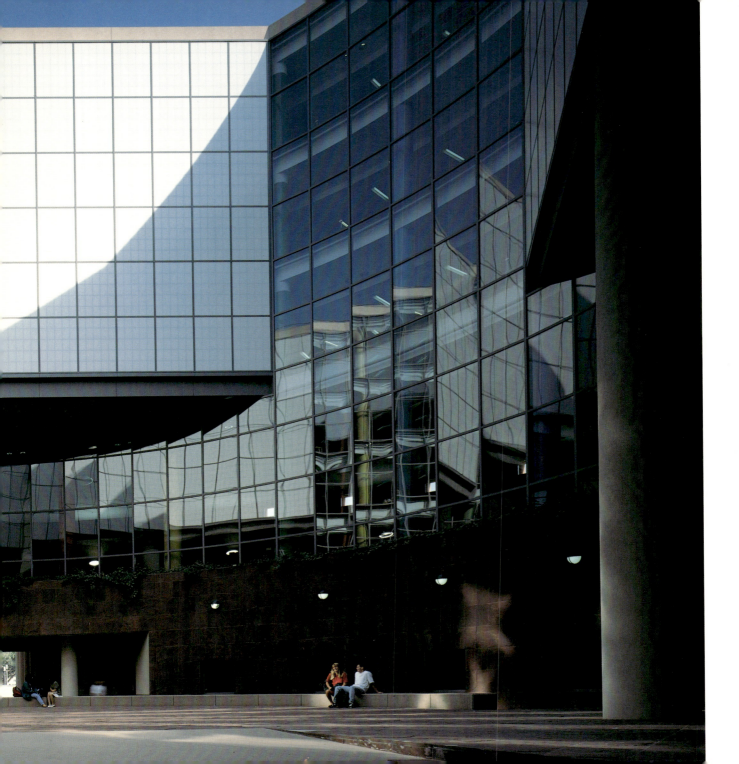

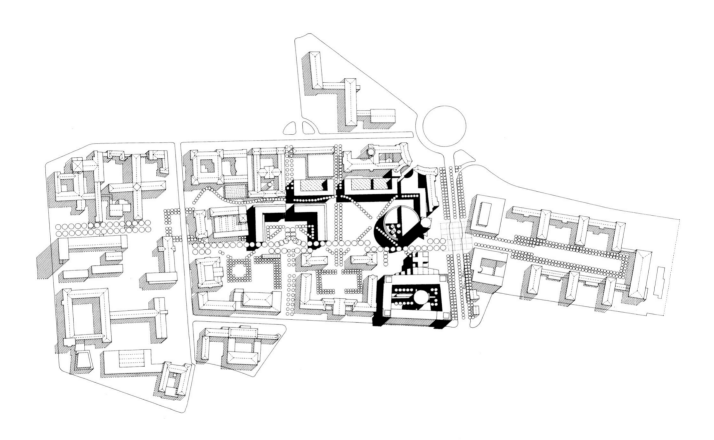

Accommodation: Expansion to the chemistry department for laboratories and offices with social rooms, library, general expansion space for other departments, classrooms, workshops, offices and a centralised lecture facility. **Schedule of net areas m²**, Total 30,200, Lecture theatre 3,000, Administration 3,000, Psychology department 5,000, Building engineering 11,000, Machine workshops 3,200, Chemistry department 5,000. **Architects**: Michael Wilford and Partners, Chris Dyson, Jeremy Emerson, David Haseler, Stuart McKnight, Ian McMillan, John Munro, Jonathan Rose, Charlie Sutherland, Simon Whiting. **Consultants**: Mechanical & Electrical Engineers: Jaeger, Mornhinweg + Partner, Stuttgart.

DRESDEN UNIVERSITY CAMPUS EXPANSION

Invited competition
1994

The campus is at the end of a major urban axis on the southern edge of the city at the junction of four urban grid patterns. It is currently sub-divided by a major street, but is without a clear primary entrance. Most buildings on Campus are haphazardly arranged, looking out onto the street and turning their backs on the centre of the campus.

A new administration tower with a circular lecture theatre cluster and plaza define a central entrance. On the major street at the intersection of the major axes to unite. The separate halves of the campus are united by locating the entrance on the main street, at the junction of the major axis. The Tower signals the presence of the Campus on the City skyline.

New linear, faculty buildings establish a series of interlocking courtyard gardens which develop existing axes into an all-embracing spatial system enclosing a central quadrangle and focused towards the entrance plaza. New geometric planting reinforces existing avenues and together with informal tree clusters establishes an individual character for each garden.

The new faculties respect the scale and materials of the existing buildings with the Tower and lecture theatre cluster surfaced in metal and glass to form 'jewels' in the architectural composition.

Shadow plan

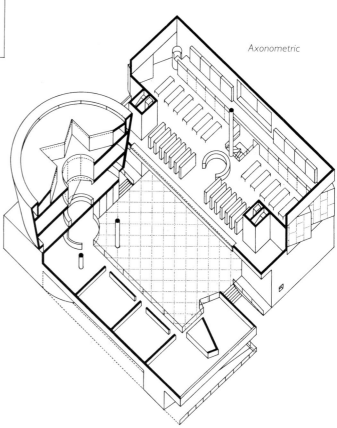

Axonometric

Accommodation: A national centre for literature, library, gallery and study centre. **Schedule of net areas m²**, total: 4,200. Special study rooms 200, Gallery 600, Shop 100, Cafe 400, Library stacks/reading (150 reader positions) 2,500, Multi-purpose room (250 seats) 400. **Architects**: Michael Wilford and Partners, Paul Barke, Chris Dyson, Liam Hennessy, Andrew Pryke, Charlie Sutherland, Gareth Wilkins. **Consultants**: Cost and Programme: Buro 4.

NATIONAL CENTRE FOR LITERATURE SWANSEA

Invited competition
1992

Ty Llen is located on a boulevard at the western edge of the town centre, as a significant public building and cultural nucleus of the City.

An enclosed public square linking two major streets provides an outdoor communal space to relax and meet friends. Entrances to Ty Llen and the City Library face each other across the Square, stimulating day and night activity. In fine weather, people would be able to move outdoors and further enliven the space. Ty Llen defines three sides of the Square and would initially overlook a garden if construction of the City Library is delayed. Top-lit exhibition galleries at first floor level extend across the boulevard frontage, with the striking form of its rotunda providing a memorable presence and encouraging cross-fertilisation of ideas amongst writers.

Within the City Library, the main entrance, exhibition area and children's library are linked by a grand stair to the music, drama and lending libraries on the first floor. They share a central reading room overlooking the Square. The stair continues to the spacious, rooflit, reference library above. A translucent wall faces the Square, expressing the book stack as a literary 'treasure house'. Reading rooms enjoy views across the Square and city skyline.

The base and flanking walls of Ty Llen are faced with Welsh slate, and the drum and gallery rooflights are clad in green pre-patinated copper.

August-Schaper-Str.

Laalzener Turm · Bei der Mühle

71.5

71

Accommodation: New railway station with adjacent mixed use development including retail, offices, business centres and residential. **Schedule of net areas m²**, total: 55,100, Station 1,200, Retail 2,200, Office 15,000, Warehousing 3,000, Workshops 4,000, Market hall 1,200, Beer garden 500, Apartments 21,000, Boarding house 7,000, 3 storey underground structure providing 25,000 m² of parking. **Architects**: Michael Wilford and Partners, Darren Capel, Iain Clavadetscher, Chris Dyson, Suzanne Garrett, Liam Hennessy, David Jennings, Christopher Matthews, Alison McLellan, Ian McMillan, John Munro, Jess Paull, Andrew Pryke , David Reat, Brian Reynolds, Manuel Schupp, Sven Schmedes, Charlie Sutherland, Simon Usher, Karen Waloschek, Ulrike Wilke. **Consultants**: Structural Engineers: Boll & Partner. Services Engineers: Jaeger, Mornhinweg & Partner, Stuttgart.

EXPO 2000 RAILWAY STATION HANNOVER

Invited competition
1995

A new railway station and raised triangular plaza containing bus and taxi drop-off with parking beneath, provides a dramatic and efficient arrival gateway for visitors arriving at the Expo by train, bus or car. A new public park accommodates large residential 'villas', office buildings and small workshops.

The plaza, which is lined with offices, hotel and information kiosks, guides visitors via generous stairs and escalators to a boulevard and elevated travelator tube. This passes between information and advertising screens, shielding the nondescript industrial hinterland from view and providing an attractive weather-protected connection to the Expo. In addition to its occasional intense transport activity, the plaza will provide a vibrant focus for the residential community.

A new railway bridge completes a perimeter ring road around the master plan area. With new internal feeder roads, it provides services access to existing buildings during Expo. New tree-lined avenues and orchards soften parking areas and extend existing green spaces.

Context plan

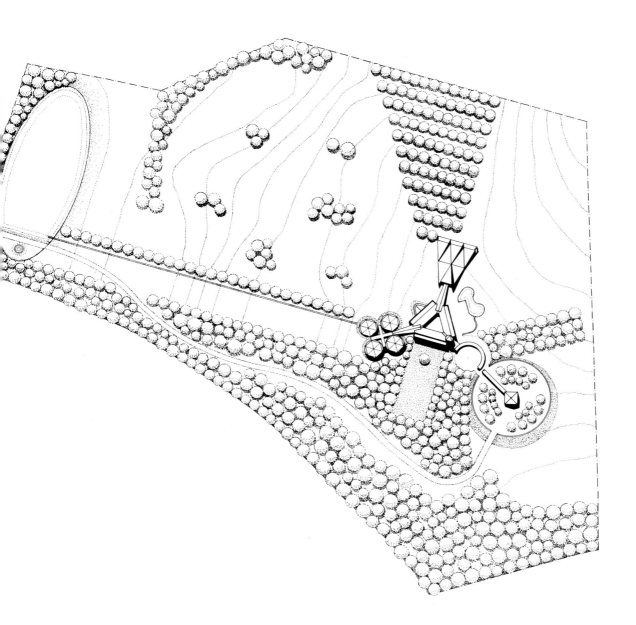

Client: Rare Limited. **Accommodation**: New headquarters for 250 staff to create video computer games with development studios, administration offices and command facilities including a sports centre and restaurant in a landscape setting. **Schedule of net areas m²**, total: 5,100, Reception/administration 1,350, Development studios 2,400, Sports facilities 1,000, Out buildings 250. **Architects**: Michael Wilford and Partners Ltd, Darren Capel, Chris Dyson, Ian McMillan, Adele Pascal, Brian Reynolds. **Consultants**: Mechanical & Electrical Engineers: E.Griffiths & Sons, Structural Engineers: Curtins, Quantity Surveyor: Derek Evans & Partners, Programme: Buro 4.

RARE LIMITED LEICESTERSHIRE

1995

Rare Limited is a computer and software development company responsible for some of the best selling computer games. The company believe the key to their success is their unique working environment in the heart of the English countryside.

Rare plan to double their staff and relocate to a new headquarters in landscaped grounds close to their present location.

The tripartite plan is centred upon a triangular cloistered courtyard building containing administration, restaurant and other shared elements of the brief, forming the central meeting and security point for staff and visitors. The main entrance, circular cluster of development offices and the tapered sports building are linked to the corners of the courtyard. The restaurant is the social hub of the headquarters with dramatic views across the surrounding landscape.

The building mass is minimised to integrate it into the existing natural habitat, with each function clearly expressed and capable of independent construction.

After several weeks of work, the client decided that our design was too radical and is now pursuing a 'traditional' solution with another architect.

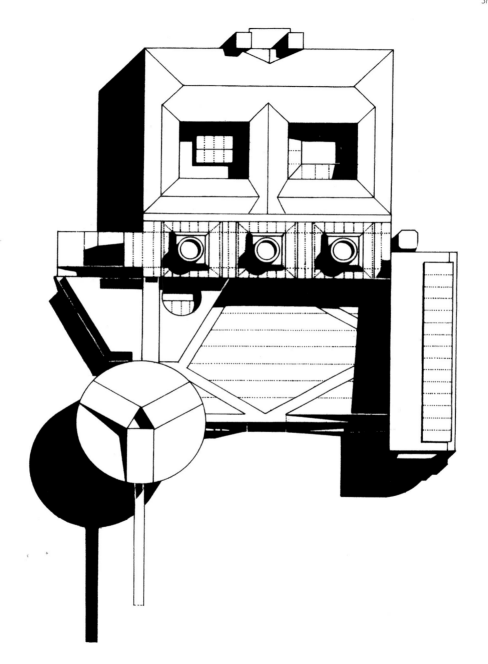

Accommodation: An extension to and re-working of the existing library to provide a new reference reading room, exhibition galleries, multi-purpose auditorium, cafe, special reading rooms for rare books, music, maps and prints, new bookstacks and information facilities. **Schedule of net areas m²**, total: 25,080. New reference reading room (2,500 seats) 4,440, Classrooms 1,150, Exhibition galleries 990, Multi-purpose auditorium 1,070, Cafe (600 seats) 500, Reading rooms, rare books, oriental and music 7,630, Maps and prints, Administration and reception of goods 1,820 + 3,420, Stock room 1,560, Security 130, External institutes 2,370, Total 25,080. **Architects**: Michael Wilford and Partners, Chris Dyson, Biork Haroldsdöttir, Andrew Pryke, Simon Whiting. **Consultants**: Library Consultant: MJ Long/Colin St Wilson and Partners. Structural Engineers: Ove Arup and Partners, M&E: Ove Arup and Partners, Quantity Surveyor: Davis Langdon and Everest, Acoustics: Arup Acoustics.

ROYAL LIBRARY EXTENSION COPENHAGEN

Open competition
1993

The eastern edge of Stotsholmen island has become a vacuous zone in need of revitalisation following the demise of maritime activity. The Library expansion provides the opportunity to establish a redevelopment plan for the entire zone.

In 1965, an office extension was built immediately against the east facade of the original 1906 Library. It forms a barrier to the extension and we propose its removal to allow appropriate connections and to restore the 1906 facade to its former stature.

The new extension responds to the form and scale of adjacent buildings and is integrated with the existing building to form a single functional entity. An elevated entrance facing a new public Plaza is located at the interface between new and existing buildings and is signalled by a projecting canopy. The circular pavilion and raised garden provide dramatic formal and spatial focuses of the composition. An Information Hall extends across the width of the new building as a tall

conservatory, at the 'piano nobile' level. This links the plaza entrance and the reference library, and combines with the main axis of the existing Library to form a 'T' shaped public circulation armature.

The conservatory, with the facade of the original building as a back drop accommodates three elevated pyramids housing special libraries, and provides dramatic river views across the garden. The information desk, situated at the centre of the 'T' is the functional heart of the Library.

Each reading room has an individual, memorable shape and is connected directly to the bookstack reservoir on the lower levels of the building. The reference library, containing multi-level reading balconies, encloses the Library garden. The conservatory is linked by colonnade to a cafe beneath the circular pavilion. The lower entrance hall, connected by a grand stair to the information hall above, leads to the exhibition galleries and a multi-purpose auditorium.

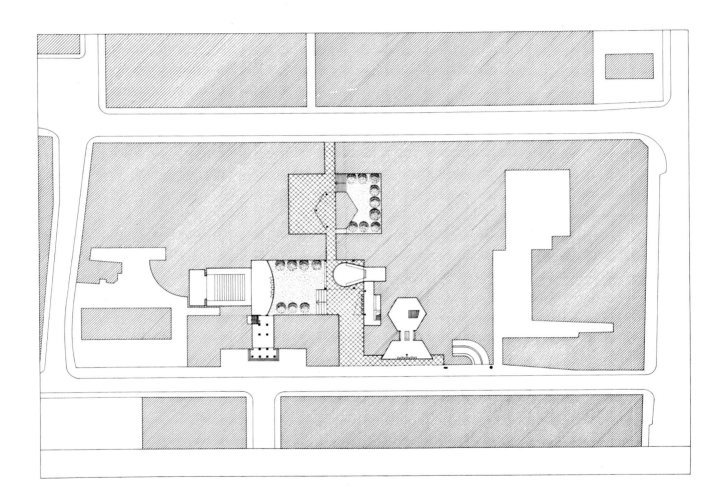

Client: Kurpfalz Carree, Cinemaxx film theatre Betriebe, Staatliches Hochbauamt und universitätsbauamt Mannheim. **Accommodation**: 10 cinemas seating 2,650 with associated foyers and offices. Practice teaching and seminar rooms, offices, chamber music and big band rehearsal rooms, café and social spaces, ballet rehearsal rooms, changing facilities, offices and social spaces. **Schedule of net areas m²**, total: 13,800. Cinemas 3,200, Front of House 1,200, Back of House 400, Restaurant 100, Music School 2,300, Ballet School 1,300, Car Park 5,300. **Architects**: Michael Wilford and Partners, London and Stuttgart. Gudrun Ahrens, Darren Capel, Stephan Gerstner, Klaus Grübnau, Mark Jeffs, Alison McLellan, Stuart McKnight, Ian McMillan, David Reat, Sven Schmedes, Manuel Schupp, Charlie Sutherland, Karen Waloschek. **Consultants**: Project Managers: BOP Gesellschaft für Bauoptimierung, Bad Soden. Mechanical & Electrical Engineers: KHS-Plan, Frankenthal. Structural: Engineers Wayss, & Freytag, Frankfurt. Acoustics: Dr. Westphal, Wachenheim. Fire Consultant: Dipl.Ing.Manfred Hass, Endingen/Neckerhaussen. Building Physics: KHS-Plan, Frankenthal. Soil Expertise: Trischler & Partner, Darmstadt.

MUSIC SCHOOL EXTENSION & CINEMAXX MANNHEIM

1995

The Music School extension and Cinemaxx are combined into a new building adjacent to the existing Music School, within the historic city centre. A circular court forms the core of the building uniting the three formal elements of the composition - L-shaped Cinemaxx, semi-circular music school and tower.

A new entrance leading to the heart of the Music School allows entry either from the street or landscaped courtyard behind the existing building. The student cafe, situated in the base of the tower, is accessed from the new entrance hall. A grand staircase leads to the Chamber Music and Big Band rooms on the piano nobile level and to Practice Studios, Seminar Rooms and Offices on four upper floors.

The tower registers the presence of the school and will form a gateway to a future pedestrian passage through the city block. It contains a stack of three double height dance studios topped by a roof terrace for outdoor performance, study and relaxation. Future development of the mid-block landscaped courtyard may include a small opera theatre.

The Cinemaxx, containing 10 cinemas on four levels, is entered directly from the street into a spacious central Foyer lit from the circular court above. A separate restaurant adjacent to the Marienstrasse entrance brings further life to the street and provides an alternative venue to the bars and concessions inside. A grand staircase climbs through all levels giving views down to the foyer below.

Although one building, each part is given its own expression through the selection of materials and colour.

Buildings and projects
James Stirling Michael Wilford and Associates

1971	Olivetti HQ, Milton Keynes	1980	Music Academy, Stuttgart
1972	Arts Centre, St Andrews University	1981	Houston Plaza, Houston
1972-77	Southgate Low Cost Housing, Runcorn New Town		(limited competition)
1975	Museum for Northrhine Westphalia, Düsseldorf (invited competition)	1983-88	Performing Arts Centre, Cornell University, USA
1975	Wallraf-Richartz Museum, Cologne (invited competition)	1983	Casalecchio New Town, Bologna
1976	Meineke Straße, Berlin	1983	Villa Lingotto, Turin (limited competition)
1976	Government Centre, Doha (limited competition)	1983	British Telecom HQ, Milton Keynes (limited competition)
1976	Regional Centre, Florence (national competition)	1983	Public Library, Latina
1977	UNEP HQ Nairobi	1984-88	Tate Gallery, Albert Dock, Liverpool
1977	Revisions to the Nolli Plan, Rome	1985	Museums of New Art and Sculpture Tate Gallery, London
1977	Dresdner Bank, Marburg	1985 –	Transport Interchange, Bilbao
1977	Housing Study for Muller Pier, Rotterdam	1985	National Gallery Extension, London (limited competition)
1977-84	State Gallery and Chamber Theatre, Stuttgart (invited competition)	1986 –	Number 1 Poultry, Mansion House London
1978	Institute of Biology and Biochemistry, Tehran	1986	Thyssen Art Gallery, Lugano (limited competition)
1978	Bayer A.G. PF Zentrum, Monheim, (limited competition)	1986-92	Braun HQ, Research and Production, Melsungen (limited competition) with Walter Nägeli
1978	11 Townhouses, New York (limited competition)	1986	Statetheatre Warehouse, Stuttgart (limited competition)
1979-81	School of Architecture extension, Rice University, Houston	1986	Paternoster Square, London (limited competition)
1979-87	Wissenschaftszentrum, Berlin (limited competition)	1986	Bracken House, London (limited competition)
1979-84	Sackler Museum, Harvard University, USA	1987	Kaiserplatz Aachen, with Marlies Hentrup and Norbert Heyers
1980	Chemistry Department, Columbia University, New York	1987-96	Music School and Theatre Academies, Stuttgart
1980-86	Clore Gallery (Turner Collection) Tate Gallery, London		

James Stirling Michael Wilford and Associates

continued

1987	Study Centre and Library/Archive, Tate Gallery, London
1987 –	Palazzo Citterio Art Gallery (Brera Museum) Milan
1988–94	Science Library, University of California at Irvine, Los Angeles
1988	Ballet/Opera House, Toronto (limited competition)
1988	Residential Development, Canary Wharf London (limited competition)
1988	Los Angeles Philharmonic Hall (limited competition)
1988 –	5-7 Carlton Gardens, London (limited competition)
1988	Stadium Development, Seville
1989	Glyndebourne Opera Extension (limited competition)
1989	Bibliotheque de France, Paris (limited competition)
1989	Compton Verney Opera House (limited competition)
1989–91	Biennale Bookshop, Venice
1989	Tokyo International Forum (limited competition)
1990	Cinema Palace Venice (limited competition) with Marlies Hentrup and Norbert Heyers
1990	Channel 4 HQ (limited competition)
1991	Kyoto Centre (limited competition)
1991–95	Temasek Polytechnic Singapore
1991	Museum of Scotland (limited competition) with Ulrike Wilke

Buildings and projects
Michael Wilford and Partners

1992 –	Passenger Interchange and Bus Station, Bilbao
1992 –	Lowry Centre, Salford
1993 –	Performing Arts Centre, Singapore
1993 –	Sto AG Factory Headquarters and Production Plant, Weizen, Germany
1993	Ty Llen National Centre for Literature, Swansea (limited competition)
1993	Royal Library Copenhagen (competition)
1993 –	Tate Gallery, Liverpool, Phase 2
1993 – 94	Clore Gallery (Turner Collection), Tate Gallery Refurbishment
1994	British Museum, Courtyard Redevelopment (limited competition)
1994 –	Sto AG New Office Building, Weizen, Germany
1994 –	Technical University, Dresden, Germany (Competition)
1994 – 94	Sto Regional Depot, Hamburg, Germany
1994 –	LIverpool Museum, National Museums and Galleries on Merseyside
1994 –	British Embassy, Berlin (Competition)
1995	Rare Headquarters, Leicestershire
1995 –	Music School and Cinemaxx, Mannheim, Germany
1995 –	Hanover/Laatzen Trade Fair Station, Hanover, Germany (Competition)

James Stiring Michael Wilford and Associates, London & Stuttgart
Michael Wilford and Partners, London & Stuttgart, Michael Wilford, Laurence Bain, Russell Bevington
Associates: Christopher Dyson, Lisa Groom, Andrew Pryke, Peter Ray, Manuel Schupp, Charlie Sutherland.

PERSONNEL

The following personnel have contributed to the exhibition projects:

Sarah Adams	Suzanne Garrett	Catherine Martin	Klaus-Jürgen Schnell
Gudrun Ahrens	Stephan Gerstner	Christopher Matthews	Manuel Schupp
Paul Barke	Christina Garcia	Alan Mee	Daniel Seibert
Kenneth Beattie	Irmgard Gassner	Gillian McInnes	Jutta Simpfendörfer
Claire Bevington	Klaus Grübnau	Stuart McKnight	Philip Smithies
Andrew Birds	Thomas Hamilton	Alison McLellan	Andy Strickland
John Bowmer	Biork Haroldsdöttir	Ian McMillan	Charlie Sutherland
Mark Bunting	David Haseler	John Munro	Joanna Sutherland
Darren Capel	Susan Haug	Esmond O'Brien	Matthias Urich
Chris Chong	Wolfgang Heckmann	Eilish O'Donnell	Simon Usher
Hilary Clarke	Liam Hennessy	Manel Pares	Richard Walker
Birgit Class	Bernd Horn	Adele Pascal	Kit Wallace
Iain Clavadetscher	Charlie Hussey	Jess Paull	Karen Waloschek
Axel Deuschle	Mark Jeffs	Richard Portchmouth	Siggi Wernik
Robert Dinse	David Jennings	Andrew Pryke	Simon Whiting
John Dorman	Daphne Kephalidis	Peter Ray	Karenna Wilford
Felim Dunne	Manfred Klemt	David Reat	Ulrike Wilke
Frances Dunne	Kirsten Lees	Brian Reynolds	Gareth Wilkins
Chris Dyson	Steffan Lehmann	Jonathan Rose	Megan Williams
Jeremy Emerson	Heike Lentz	Leandro Rotondi	Denis Wolf
Jürgen Engelhardt	Toby Lewis	Mike Russum	Gary Wyatt
Klaus Fischer	Karin Ludewig	John Ryan	Eric Yim
Michelle Floyd	Tessa Mahoney	Ulli Schaad	
Kenny Fraser	Markus Mangold	Sven Schmedes	

Music School Stuttgart

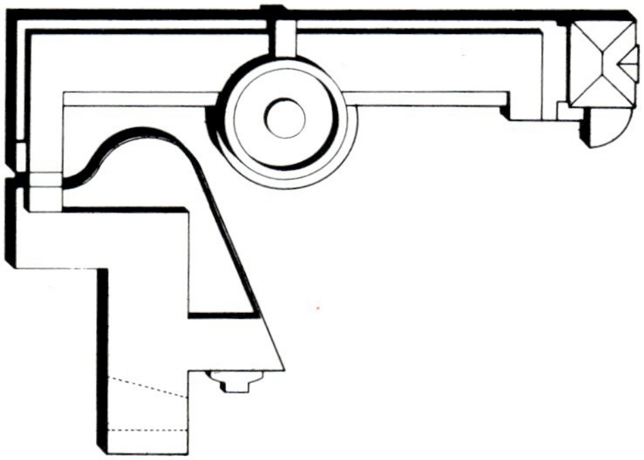

Expo 2000 Railway
Station Hannover

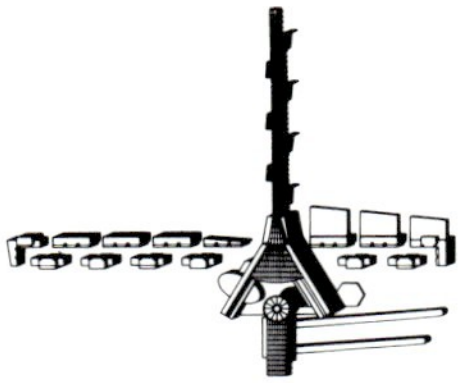

Royal Library Extension
Copenhagen

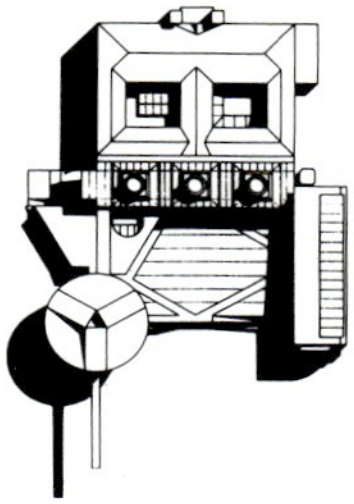

Dresden University
Campus Expansion

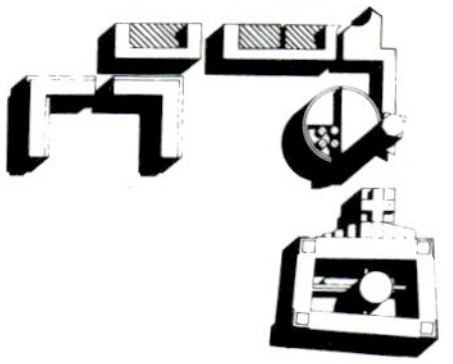

Science Library U.C. Irvine

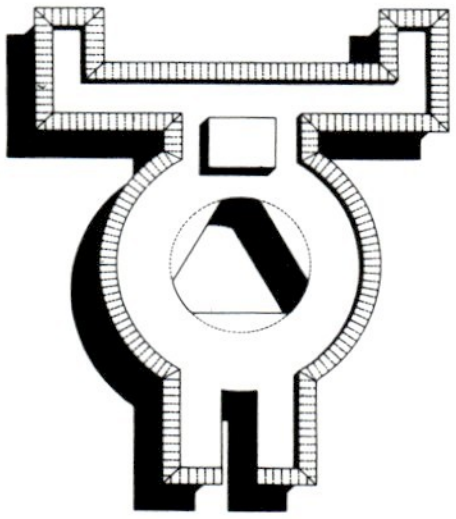

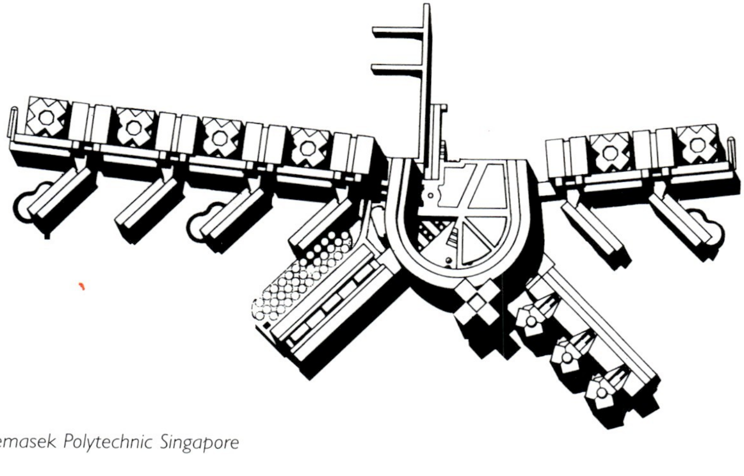

Temasek Polytechnic Singapore

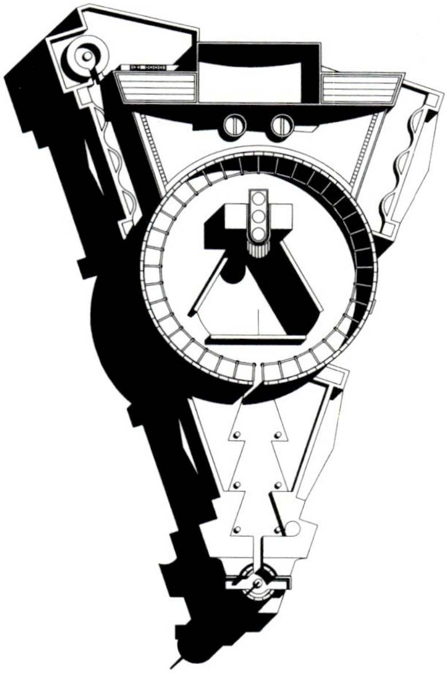

Number 1 Poultry London

National Centre for
Literature Swansea

Rare Headquarters
Leicestershire

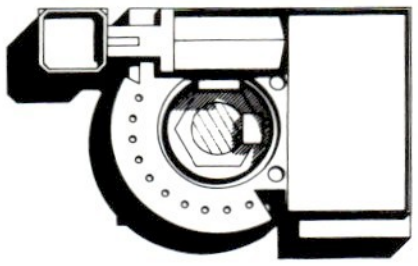

Music School Extension
& Cinemaxx Mannheim

Sto Depot Hamburg

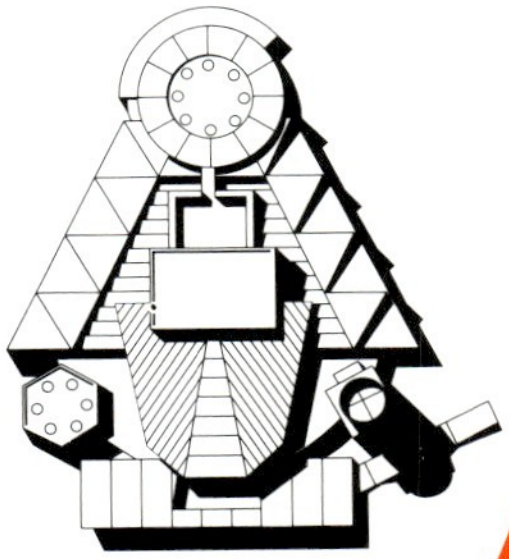

Lowry Centre Salford

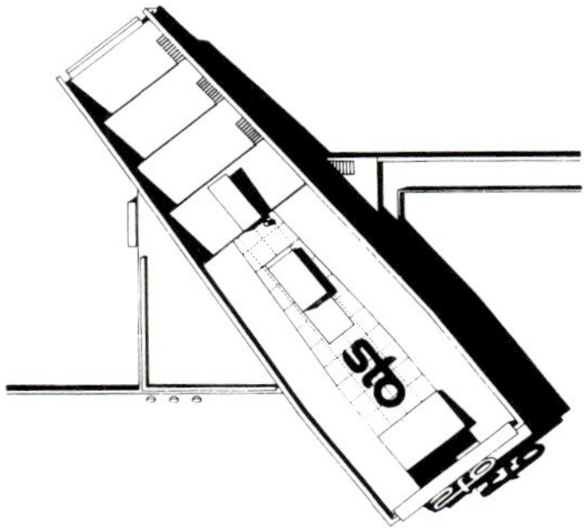

Sto Communications Weizen

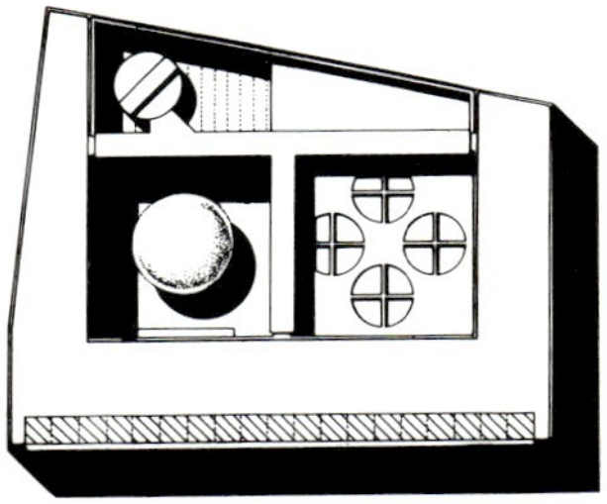

British Embassy Berlin

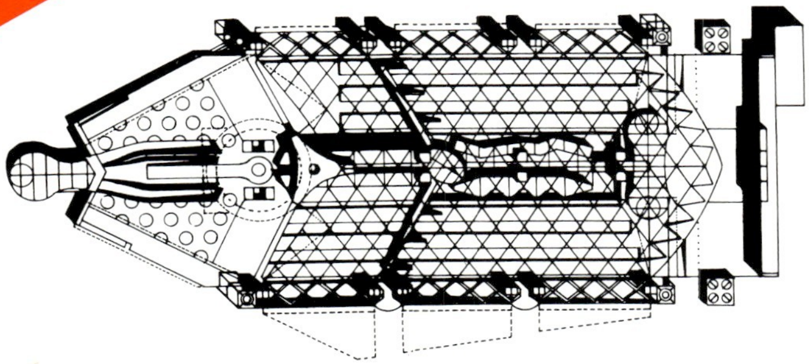

Abando Interchange Bilbao

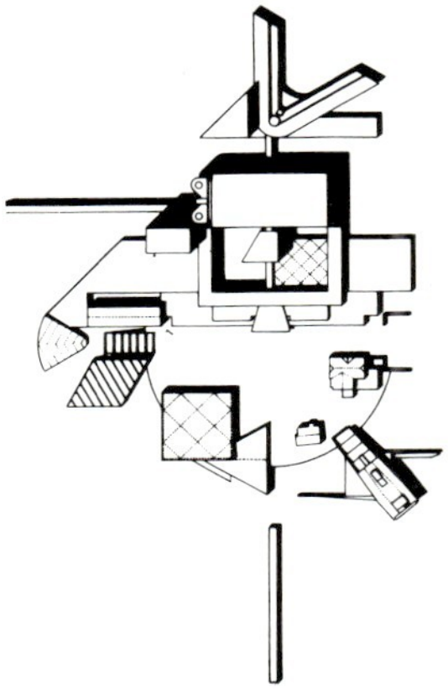

Sto Headquarters Masterplan Weizen

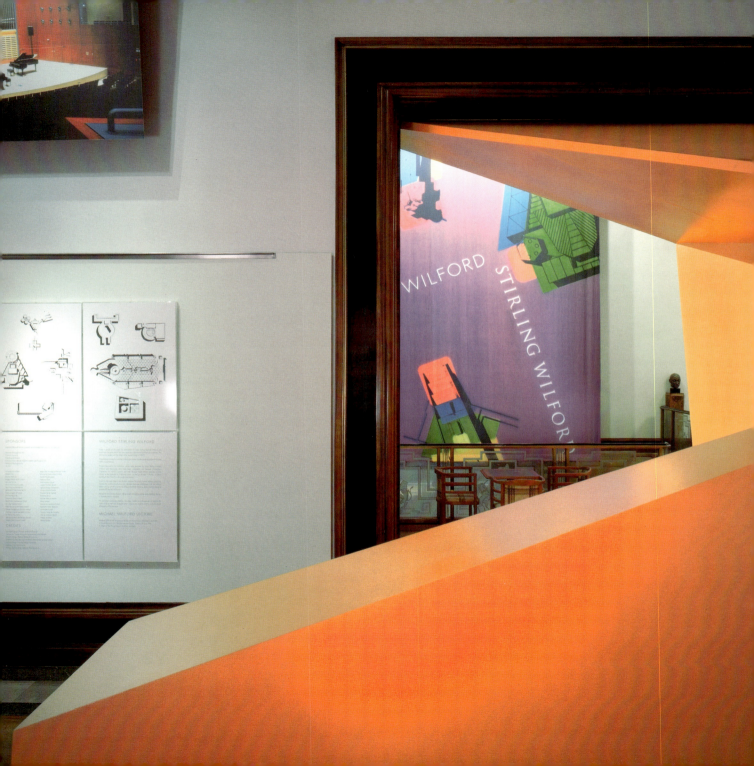

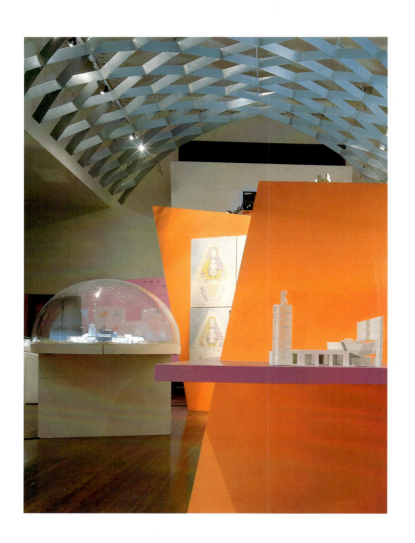

SALFORD

BRITISH EMBASSY BERLIN

BRITISH EMBA

Michael Wilford & Partners gratefully acknowledge the support of our sponsors:

Advanta Management AG
Concord Sylvania
Ove Arup & Partners
Estación Intermodal de Abando Gestion del Proyecto S.A.
Sarkpoint Reprographics
Sto AG

Acoustiguide Ltd
Atelier One
Barclays Bank plc
Bingdon Restoration Ltd
Boll und Partner
Bovis Construction Ltd
Buro Happold Partnership
Büromarkt Streit
Davis Langdon & Everest
DP Architects Pte
Executive Travel Ltd
Feicht Natursteinbetrieb GmbH
Dr.- Ing. Manfred Flohrer
FSB Franz Schneider Brakel GmbH
Gleeds Management Services Ltd
Gormley (Marble Specialists) Ltd
Ian Martin Associates
IBB Ingenieurbüro Burrer und Partner
Ibstock Hathernware Ltd
Jaeger Mornhinweg und Partner GmbH
John Laing Construction Ltd
Kandor Modelmakers
Kjelstrup Olsen
Kurpfalz Carree GbR
Lauster Steinbau GmbH
Lighting Design Partnership
London Graphic Centre
Mackrell Turner Garrett
McKenna & Co
Metallbau Hirsch
Michael Weiss & Partner
Minet Ltd
PLANoffice
Solonia Sonnenschutz GmbH
Staniforth Public Relations
StoVerotec GmbH
Thomas Manss & Co
Werner Schwarz GbmH
Whelan & Grant
Whitby & Bird

Photography: Richard Bryant, p22, 35, 38, 42, 43, 46, 47, 50, 58, 59, 114, 119, 122, 123, 162, 167, 170, 171, 174, 175, 178, 179. 198, 199, 200, 201, 202, 203, 204, 205, 206, 207. Bundesarchiv Koblenz, p133 (upper left). Martin Charles, p6. John Donat, p60, 63, 66, 68, 69. Chris Edgecombe, p10, 34 (upper right, lower left and right), 74, 78, 82, 86, 87, 98, 106, 107, 110, 111, 126, 130, 142, 143, 146, 150, 151, 154, 155, 158. Marianne Götz, p34 (upper left). O.L.M., p133 (upper right). Singapore Piling and Civil Engineering Pte Ltd, p44. Manfred Stock, p27. **Models**: Music School, Stuttgart, Kurtz Ritznann. Number One, Poultry, Kandor Modelmakers (p60 & 63), Morris Associates (p66, 68 & 69). Lowry Centre, Salford, Kandor Modelmakers. Abando Interchange, Bilbao, Kandor Modelmakers. Sto Communications, Weizen, Kandor Modelmakers. British Embassy, Berlin, Kandor Modelmakers.